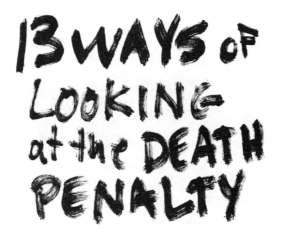

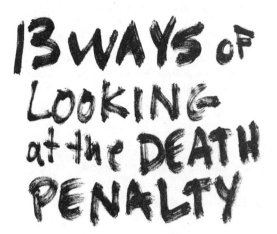

13 WAYS of LOOKING at the DEATH PENALTY

Mario Marazziti

Afterword by Paul Elie

Seven Stories Press

NEW YORK • OAKLAND

A Seven Stories Press First Edition

Seven Stories Press
140 Watts Street
New York, NY 10013
www.sevenstories.com

College professors may order examination copies of Seven Stories Press titles for free. To order, visit http://www.sevenstories.com/textbook or send a fax on school letterhead to (212) 226-1411.

Library of Congress Cataloging-in-Publication Data
Marazziti, Mario, author.
13 ways of looking at the death penalty / Mario Marazziti ; afterword by Paul Elie.
pages cm
ISBN 978-1-60980-567-8 (hardback)
1. Capital punishment. I. Title. II. Title: Thirteen ways of looking at the death penalty.
K5104.M37 2015
364.66--dc23
2014043858

Printed in the United States
9 8 7 6 5 4 3 2 1

Contents

1.
Introduction

At long last, I was in San Francisco—and it was there, in the city named for St. Francis of Assisi, that I heard the news that finally made me certain that new life was still possible.

It was November 2000 and I was there for the first time, staying at a hotel called the Cathedral Hill on Van Ness, corner of Geary, for what at that time was the largest-ever gathering of anti-death penalty advocates in the US. Lance Lindsey, then the executive director of Death Penalty Focus, was there; and Richard Dieter, who runs the Death Penalty Information Center; and Sister Helen Prejean, the activist nun portrayed by Susan Sarandon in *Dead Man Walking*. With my friends in the Community of Sant'Egidio in Rome, I had become active in efforts against the death penalty. We had collected three million signatures in 152 countries calling for a worldwide moratorium. I had become acquainted with Sister Helen and through her had wound up here, as a speaker representing Europe to the National Coalition to Abolish the Death Penalty conference. I had to explain to an audience used to failure and small numbers how we had managed to collect three million signatures: "You need a pen, and it takes a lot of work," I would say. There was nothing mysterious about it.

I was due to speak in a final session about strategies and the future. But something else was on my mind. At six o'clock that evening, a man I knew was scheduled to die at the age of forty-four—a man I had come to think of as a real friend, even as family, even though he and I had never met. His name was John Paul Penry.

Penry had been on death row in Texas ever since his conviction in 1980 for the rape and murder of a young woman named Pamela Mosley Carpenter in Livingston, East Texas—the very place where Texas's death row was located. In 1989 the Supreme Court had reversed the sentence because of an apparent flaw in the case. Then Penry was retried and sentenced to death a second time. As the plane from Rome landed in San Francisco, the Texas Board of Pardons and Paroles had voted—sixteen to one—against commuting Penry's sentence to life without parole and granting him a reprieve. Now it was time for the Texas justice system to carry out the death sentence the parole board had demanded.

The only problem was that they were executing a man who at the age of forty-four still believed in Santa Claus—a man whose IQ tests ranged between fifty-three and sixty, far below the threshold of what is called "intellectual disability."

How had Penry's life become intertwined with mine?

My friend Gianni Guidotti, who is a doctor in Rome, had become pen pals with him, which gradually became more possible as others on death row helped Penry to write. I was reminded of some drawings Penry had sent us, so similar to my own childhood artwork: a car, a truck, a schematic house—were they third-grade, second-grade, first-grade level? Really, was the world going to be better off after eliminating our friend John?

I had already spoken to Gianni once from the conference. He had gone from Rome to Texas to meet Penry in Livingston before Penry's transfer, on the very last day, to Huntsville, where he was to be executed. Gianni had spoken with him, played with him, but it was hard for him to dispel the tension that Penry could perceive perfectly well. Penry was scared and desperate, Gianni told me in a phone call; he did not want to be "put to sleep."

The second time Gianni and I spoke that day was considerably different. Gianni could hardly speak, but I understood from his joy what had happened: just three hours before he was set to die by lethal injection, Penry was given a thirty-day stay of execution pending a decision by the Supreme Court concerning a full review of the case. He had already ordered a double cheeseburger as his last meal when the news came. He never got his burger, because when the stay arrived he was immediately taken back to Livingston.

Since I was probably the first person at the conference to know that Penry had gotten a reprieve, I hastened to tell the others: Lance, and Richard, and Sister Helen, and Abraham Bonowitz from Amnesty International and the Ohio-based Movement, and a married couple from Texas, parents of a death-row inmate—their son, they told me, had been one of those who'd taught Penry to read a little and to write his own name. I vividly remember the joy of one woman, a pastor involved in "restorative justice," who said, "Revenge is steady and stubborn, but stupid. That is why we will win."

The next day, to conclude the conference, we marched through the streets of San Francisco, hundreds of us, each with a poster or a flag, our signs held high so that people in their cars could read them and the cable car drivers could ring their bells in support.

We marched to the pier and onto the boat that would take us to San Quentin, the site of the largest death row in America, so near to mythic San Francisco. It staggered the mind to think that the same place that gave the world Beat poetry, the Summer of Love, and psychedelic rock persists in practicing capital punishment more aggressively than most countries in the world, more so even than the world's police states and dictatorships—even as the rest of the world is turning away from the death penalty once and for all.

It was cold and clear that day, and I was sure it'd be colder inside the prison walls. I hoped that the prisoners could hear us inside. I hoped that somehow our efforts would help to humanize the law enforcement and prison staff—all those people involved in the dehumanization process that is called "capital punishment" or "the death penalty."

—◦—

All over the globe—in some countries more than others, to be sure—people are realizing that the state-sponsored killing of people is not worthy of our common humanity.

When the Helsinki Conference on Security and Cooperation in Europe took place in 1975—an early sign of the easing of the Cold War and the strengthening of international cooperation—just sixteen countries had abolished the death penalty or committed to doing so.

By the time the Berlin Wall came down in 1989, there were nineteen more. The most prominent example was France, where in 1981 François Mitterand and Robert Badinter, just elected president and minister of justice respectively, took the country directly from the use of the guillotine to a radical rejection of death as punishment, abolishing it in all cases.

The next year alone—1990—nine more countries abolished the death penalty. By 2000, twenty nine more countries had done so, including Albania, the states of the former Yugoslavia, and the Baltic republics.

Most recently (I write in late 2014), Latvia and Poland have ratified a binding international Covenant. One hundred and five of the 192 countries represented at the United Nations have abolished the death penalty by law, and another forty-three have abolished it in practice—either through public moratoria or by the *de facto* moratorium that can be counted when a country declines to practice capital punishment for a decade or longer.

The countries that have abandoned the death penalty range from Gabon to Mongolia, from the United Kingdom to Argentina, from Cambodia to South Africa and to Russia. Some have outlawed the death penalty for the first time; others, having outlawed it decades ago, have taken resolutions never to adopt it in the future. The countries that still employ the death penalty— among them Saudi Arabia, Iran, Iraq, Egypt, Somalia, China, Japan, and the United States—are seen as outliers and strange bedfellows.

By now, the Community of Sant'Egidio together with other groups including the World Coalition Against the Death Penalty have collected more than five million signatures. In 2007 the General Assembly of the UN made a resolution affirming, for the first time, that executions must be stopped and that capital punishment is wrong, and declaring the worldwide goal of ending the death penalty forever.

In many respects this movement has left the United States behind. In the US, thirty-four states still have the death penalty on the books—"retentionist," we call them. Sixteen states have carried out a death sentence in the past three years. Seven states executed at least one person in 2013. Texas and California are the leaders: Texas carries out more executions than any other American state, while California sentences people to death in numbers that—thankfully—far outstrip its capacity and its will to execute them, with the effect that nearly 750 people currently languish on its death row. In July 2014, Federal Judge Cormac J. Carney wrote that lengthy and unpredictable delays have resulted in an arbitrary and unfair capital punishment system.

But public opinion in the United States is turning. NGOs, citizens' groups, progressive politicians, and religious people have inspired popular opposition to the death penalty, so that many American cities and states are now anti-death-penalty zones: not just Cambridge and Berkeley, but New Jersey, Connecticut, Illinois, Maryland, and New Mexico. The New Hampshire Senate voted 12–12 on a bill to repeal the death penalty on April 17, 2014. In 2013, the majority of senators in Nebraska supported repealing the death penalty in a test vote, but the bill was later filibustered. In Delaware, the bill to repeal the death penalty is currently stalled, while Colorado's bill was withdrawn in 2013. That same year, an attempt to reintroduce capital punishment in Massachusetts was defeated. It is fair to say that opposition to the death penalty in America is stronger now than at any point since the courts re-legalized it in 1973.

The movement for abolition has taken place largely out of the view of most Americans. Attention in the US has focused instead on narrow technical questions related to the death penalty: Is it legal? Is it discriminatory? Is it cost-effective? Is it a real deterrent to violent crime?

But the movement is strong, and it is getting stronger by the day.

◄○►

My first memory of the death penalty is from 1960, when I was eight years old. In California, a man named Caryl Chessman was fighting the justice system without a lawyer—playing chess with the state. He had written several books, and his fame was such that *Time* magazine put his picture on its cover and the Italian papers were following his story in the days leading up to his execution. When Chessman was put to death, the news story I read about it included some sketches: the gas chamber, how it works, the poison pill sent from the top to a basin with water, the gas starting, the condemned man choking. I do not have many memories from those years, which were difficult ones in my life, but I still remember those sketches of a man dying in a gas chamber.

A few years later I joined a group of students who had begun to meet at the Chiesa Nuova, an old and much-loved Borromini church in the center of Rome, at the initiative of Andrea Riccardi, a student at the Virgilio, a nearby high school. One thing led to another, and the Community of Sant'Egidio was formed, named after an abandoned convent in Rome that later became our headquarters. Over the years, and then the decades, the community took root in local communities in over seventy countries. We saw the spread of violence in the big cities of the West and the Global South; we saw the destructive power of the various clans of organized crime, from the *camorra* to the *maras.* And we sought solutions. As we witnessed new friends becoming victims in civil wars, we participated in efforts to bring about reconciliation and peace in many countries of the world, and successfully brokered peace accords from Mozambique to Guatemala, from Burundi to the Ivory Coast, from Liberia to the Balkans, and from Kosovo to the Congo and El Salvador. We helped bring about a lasting "preventive peace" after a series of coups in Niger and the end of dictatorship in Guinea-Conakry. And today a similar effort is being made in Central Africa, in Mali, and in Senegal in the Casamance region, where one of the longest local African wars has been raging for decades. Most recently, we contributed to the peace agreement that stopped a forty-year conflict in Mindanao, the Philippines, between Christians and Muslim rebels. We sought to make the Community of Sant'Egidio a point of reference for reflection on the many forms of violence prevailing in our time—from poverty to genocide—and sought to use dialogue as a tool in areas where "realism" had turned to skepticism and finally to resignation.

Naturally, our attention turned to capital punishment.

We wanted to do away with the "culture of death." And it became clear to us that the best way to reduce violence in society was to abolish the death penalty.

Capital punishment is the culmination of violence at both ends of society: the violence of the individual criminal, who is caught in a cycle of violence and whose life ends in a violent death; and the violence of the state, with its police forces and wars whose ultimate expression is the use of violent death as a form of retributive justice. In the middle, there is pain and sorrow for the families of the victims and of those who are sentenced to death, and for all the people with roles to play in the execution process. At the end of the day, capital punishment is a prison for the individual and society alike.

The death penalty is ineffective as a deterrent for crime, though it can be used very effectively as a way for religious majorities to oppress minorities, eliminate political adversaries, create terror, and spread worldwide propaganda, as ISIS has shown when it makes headlines across the globe with its beheadings in Syria and Iraq. It is not a tool of justice because it always affects religious, social, racial and ethnic minorities in unjust, disproportionate ways. It is a form of torture in the way it forces the condemned to ponder the end of his or her life, often for years, before it finally comes. It lowers all society to the level of the killer, and does not restore life to the victim, but compounds one death with another. It is a sanction that cannot be fixed if unjustly applied.

It is a legitimization of the culture of death from the highest level of worldly authority.

But isn't the execution of heinous criminals the least we can do for their victims? I remember the comment of a ten-year-old boy: "*They're going to kill him because he killed somebody, so when they kill him, who do we get to kill?*" Direct and personal contact with prisoners, executioners, and the families of victims and executed convicts, both innocent and guilty, has led us at the Community of Sant'Egidio to the conviction that the death penalty is not merely unnecessary in light of the alternative instruments of punishment and justice available. In truth, it is not itself an instrument of justice at all; it is a grave weakness in a system of justice that should preserve its rehabilitative intent, free of the primitive need for revenge and retribution. It winds up being not only a violation of human life, but a humiliation for everybody: a murder in circumstances in which the concept of legitimate defense cannot be invoked because of the disproportionate forces involved (the state on one side, a prisoner who is not in a position to harm others on the other), and because of the distance in time between the crime or presumed crime and the proposed execution. As a matter of fact, when the state kills a serial killer, *it* becomes a killer.

It seems clear to us that capital punishment is a practice to be overcome in the history of mankind, as slavery has been largely overcome. It's possible to envision a world in which capital punishment no longer exists.

◄○►

In Rome, where I live, the Coliseum is a symbol of our history, but it is also a symbol of the death penalty. There the early Christians were subjected to capital punishment by the imperial Roman authorities, left to the lions, reduced before the crowd to a bloody spectacle.

One night in 1999, the Coliseum was lit up. Albania had abolished the death penalty, and some of us in the Community of Sant'Egidio got the idea to mark this turn of events through the lighting of the landmark. Our idea (a joint venture with the mayor of Rome, Francesco Rutelli, and a UN representative, Staffan de Mistura) was to use the lighting of the Coliseum as a tool in a worldwide campaign against the death penalty. Since that night the Coliseum has been lit up several dozen times more, including when the governor of Illinois commuted the sentences of all the state's death row prisoners in 2003, and when the states of New Jersey, Connecticut, Illinois, Maryland, and New Mexico repealed their capital punishment laws.

We hope that the Coliseum will keep on being lit up regularly until the death penalty is abolished everywhere. But for now there is the more modest effort of this book, which is meant to symbolize in a different way the world's turning against the death penalty—and to suggest different ways for our society to move a little closer to the goal of a world where capital punishment is seen as the practice of an earlier, crueler time.

2.
Facts and Figures

Research provided by Bela Shayevich and Matthew Blake

14   Age of George Stinney, the youngest person to be executed in the United States in the twentieth century, at the time of his execution[1]

83   Number of days between his arrest and his execution in 1944[2]

5,757 Average number of days between sentencing and execution in 2012[3]

2005   Year when United States Supreme Court declared executing defendants who had committed their crimes as juveniles unconstitutional[4]

40   Percentage of juveniles on death row who in a 1988 study reported they had been physically and/or sexually abused[5]

0   Number of the juries who had heard the juveniles' histories of abuse, serious central nervous system injuries, and mental health[6]

11.5   Percentage of individuals executed between 1608 and 2002 whose occupation was listed as "slave," the most commonly listed occupation[7]

68   Number whose occupation was listed as "pirate"[8]

2   Number listed as "playboy"[9]

15   Number of people executed in the US between 1608 and 2002 for "sodomy, buggery, or bestiality"[10]

51   Number executed for horse stealing[11]

63   Percentage of white Americans who said they favored the death penalty for convicted murderers in 2013[12]

36   Percentage of African-Americans who said they favored the death penalty in the same survey[13]

3   Factor by which jurors in Washington state were found to be more likely to recommend the death sentence for a black defendant than for a white defendant in a similar case[14]

33   Percentage of Boston residents who said they supported a death sentence for Dzhokhar Tsarnaev if he were convicted of the Boston Marathon bombing[15]

76 Percentage of 2010 US executions that took place in the South[16]

0 Percentage that took place in the Northeast[17]

46 Rank of Texas among states in money spent on mental health treatment, including services in jails and prisons, in 2003[18]

32 Number of states with the death penalty in 2013[19]

10 Number of states where death row inmates were allowed contact with their families[20]

1 Number of states that do not provide access to television for death row inmates[21]

41 Percentage of 2013 US executions that took place in Texas[22]

3 Factor by which a death penalty case exceeds the cost of imprisonment in a single cell for forty years, in Texas[23]

$3,406 Cost of "tent lease and media supplies" for a 2011 execution in Idaho[24]

$165,351 Cost of remodeling the building in preparation for the execution[25]

$15 Price cap for last meals on death row in Oklahoma[26]

2011 Year Texas stopped offering last meals before executions[27]

11 Number of moans the Associated Press counted during the botched 1983 execution of Jimmy Lee Gray, at which it was later reported that the executioner, Barry Bruce, was drunk[28]

3 Number of people in the US executed by firing squad since 1976[29]

1878 Year the Supreme Court determined that drawing and quartering, public dissection, burning alive, and disembowelment were "cruel and unusual" punishment[30]

1 Number of countries that allow execution by beheading[31]

1 Number of countries that allow execution by electrocution[32]

4 Number of countries that carried out the death penalty for rape in 2013[33]

13 Number of countries that carried out executions for drug-related offenses in the same year[34]

2   States that have authorized capital punishment for drug trafficking[35]

1936 Year of the last public execution in the United States[36]

1868 Year Britain outlawed public execution[37]

1999 Year Britain formally abolished death penalty[38]

4   Number of countries that carried out public executions in 2013[39]

2   Number of executions ever recorded on video in the US[40]

38   Percentage of death row inmates found to be illiterate in 2000[41]

22   Percentage of death row inmates in 2009 that were married[42]

9:20 Ratio of women to men executed in the American colonies between 1608 and 1649[43]

1:100 approx. Ratio of women to men executed in the United States between 1950 and 2002[44]

1,640 Number of 2007 intimate partner homicides in which women were killed by their male partners (out of a total of 2,340 intimate partner homicides)[45]

55 Percentage of women on death row who reported suffering regular ongoing abuse[46]

5 Number of countries where it is illegal to sentence women to death[47]

40 Days after giving birth that a woman can legally be executed in Morocco[48]

1 Number of countries where it is legal to execute a pregnant woman[49]

193 United Nations member states as of 2012[50]

174 UN member states that were "execution-free" in 2012[51]

4,942 Number of US death row inmates between 1973 and 2009[52]

416 Number of US death row inmates between 1973 and 2009 who died by means other than execution[53]

57 Number of recorded suicides on death row in the US between 1977 and 1999[54]

144 Number of people in twenty-five states who have

been released from death row because they were found innocent[55]

85   Percentage of those death row inmates who did not legally appeal their death sentences between 1977 and 2005 who were white males[56]

45   Percentage of white males among all death row inmates in this period[57]

1/4   Chances that a Kentucky attorney representing an individual facing the death penalty would later be disbarred or resign rather than face disbarment, according to a 1994 survey[58]

$11.75   Estimated amount per hour that death penalty lawyers provided by the state in Mississippi were paid according to a 1994 survey[59]

$400   Amount defense attorney Mark O'Mara charged per hour to represent George Zimmerman, the Florida man charged with the murder of Trayvon Martin in 2012[60]

$2.5 million   Approximate total George Zimmerman owes O'Mara in legal fees[61]

35 years   Longest period of incarceration for an individual later exonerated by DNA evidence[62]

$1.75 million   Amount the state of Florida owes James Bain, a fifty-four-year-old man freed in 2009 after thirty-five years proclaiming his innocence on death row—$50,000 for each year served in prison[63]

75   Estimated percentage of overturned death penalty cases where individuals are wrongfully convicted through eyewitness misidentification[64]

3   Percentage of eyewitnesses in overturned death penalty cases who claimed to be "hypnotized" at the time of making their identifications[65]

3.
Texas, Capital of the Death Penalty

Some of the people I meet in the United States think it's strange that an Italian would have friends on death row—friends I correspond with, exchange family photographs and gifts with, and travel to America to visit. Well, I don't think it's strange to have friends on death row in America. In Italy, we think it's strange that there is a death penalty in America—that the United States, a place so advanced in so many ways, is in this way so far behind the curve of human dignity, which has been turning gradually away from capital punishment ever since the state of Tuscany abolished the death penalty in 1786. You have only to go to the Texas State Penitentiary at Huntsville to see how truly strange the death penalty is.

By the time I went to visit John Paul Penry in Livingston, Texas, he had spent half of his life on death row, and his was the only case in the history of the death penalty in the United States to be overturned by the Supreme Court or see the death sentence annulled three separate times.

He had been arrested after a woman from a prominent family was found raped and bleeding. She was taken to the hospital but did not survive. John Paul Penry was found on a bicycle, pedaling past—allegedly trying to escape. He signed a confession, although he didn't know how to read and write.

By the time I met him more than twenty years later, he was very good at drawing trucks and small houses with smoke coming from the chimneys—the kind of drawings made by seven-year-olds. Other prisoners had taught him how to write his name. When answering a letter he would usually speak his thoughts out loud while another inmate wrote them down.

He knew how to take care of himself. His hair had turned gray in prison and his face was a sort of chubbier, older version of Clark Kent's, with old-fashioned heavy spectacles, and a nice smile. He told me that someone had sent him the gift of "a big book with all the words inside it"—a dictionary. When I asked him what he meant, he pronounced the first letters on the cover of the big book—"W", "E", "B"—and when I said the word "Webster's", he was visibly happy and kept repeating, "Yes, Web—b-ster's!" with some difficulties on the "b". And he eventually gave me his review of the book: "Whoever wrote that book must have known a lot of things!" It was a good review coming from a person with the mental ability of a six- or eight-year-old.

This is the man whom the State of Texas tried to execute four times, more than anyone else in US history, with his case going back to trial each time the sentence was annulled by the higher courts. It did so even after 2002, when the Supreme Court declared the execution of intellectually disabled people unconstitutional—so that Penry's lawyers decided it was wiser to have him plead guilty and have his death sentence commuted to life than to go to trial a fourth time.

―◦―

When I entered Texas's death row for the first time I didn't yet realize how strongly the wish for *vendetta*, revenge, rather than justice, shapes death penalty cases. Penry's story made this clear. And I knew that the prosecution's wish to administer death as a punishment is only comprehensible as "retribution" pure and simple, as if there cannot be any other form that justice can take.

In Texas, the idea of retribution is typical. There are obvious connections between slavery, and the role that it played in the Southern states of the Union, and the emergence of Texas as the capital of the retributive prison system. All the innovations in the system—from the privatization of prison construction and management to the practice of execution by lethal injection—were worked out in Texas first. The result is that the country's second-largest state in terms of geographical area is also the one that has come to stand for using the instruments of justice to legitimize a culture of death rather than one of life.

The Texas prison system is mythic in size, with 187,000 prisoners and "more than twice as many paid employees as Google" (as Robert Perkinson puts it in *Texas Tough*). The current leader of the incarceration industry was actually the last Southern state to build its own penitentiary, in part because in Texas, as in other Southern states, retributive justice was understood as a personal matter rather than one involving the state. The oldest detainee is Estanislao Colon, ninety-three, paying his sentence in Young Unit, Dickinson. Texas now has the largest prison system in the United States, with a budget that ballooned from $20 million in 1965 to $2.6 billion in 2005, while the prison population grew by 1,300 percent. And the budget keeps growing. In 2010 the state also had $782.9 million in prison-related expenses outside the department's budget, making the cost of Texas's prisons $3.3 billion that year.

At least eight hundred thousand people are under supervision by the state's criminal justice apparatus in Texas, in jail, on probation, or in juvenile detention—a higher percentage of the state population, or of the nation's overall incarcerated population, than anywhere else.

—<o>—

A ninety-minute drive from Livingston is Huntsville, which has the oldest prison in the state, founded by Sam

Houston. This place is nicknamed "The Walls." Here, on the edge of a college town, there is a very different kind of campus for the more than ten thousand inmates. The Walls employs two out of three local residents. The prison boasts a brand-new museum, fronted by a sentry box, just like those of real prisons. In the gift shop, a video tells the story of the Texas penitentiary system, explains the reform of the system (which, at its beginnings, carried out the death penalty as a supposedly more civilized alternative to public lynchings), and presents photographs and objects that constitute a history of crime and its suppression: chains, handcuffs, weapons, arms manufactured in prison for an escape. Sparky—the facility's real electric chair, now retired from active service—holds a special place. The burnt American flag left on the ground during the clash among demonstrators at Gary Graham's execution lies close to the three syringes and IV tubes used in the first lethal injection execution in American history.

The mission of the museum is:

- To collect, preserve, and maintain prison artifacts, documents, oral histories, photographs, and all prison museum collections.
- To publicize and showcase the history and culture of Texas's prison system in order to attract visitors to the museum annually and to enhance learning.
- To maintain fiscal accountability for the

operation, maintenance, and expansion of the Texas Prison Museum, Inc.
- To operate, maintain, and expand quality made properties.

Online, there is a Yelp review of the museum: "Something to do for an hour and better than expected. Can't beat that for $4."

—<o>—

Jim Willett is the museum's director. He's a serene and cheerful man with blue eyes. He formerly served as warden at the Walls, whose death chamber has administered the highest number of lethal injections in the United States since 1982. At the time of our meeting it wasn't hard to imagine that Texas would be the first US state to exceed five hundred executions. (It did, in 2013.)

Willett's eyes are the eyes of someone who watched firsthand the July 1974 massacre that took place after drug lord Fred Gomez Carrasco's attempted escape. Lengthy negotiations did not suffice: in the end the hostages were all killed.

Rage over the Carrasco uprising convinced even a gentle religious man like Rev. Carroll Pickett of the need for retributive justice. In 1982 Pickett, a Presbyterian minister, became the first chaplain to assist at executions by lethal injection and to console the death row inmate on his last day of life. When I met Pickett in Conroe, between Houston and Huntsville, he, too, couldn't shake that experience. He had escorted ninety-five people to their deaths—heard their last words, their confessions, their fears, their protestations of innocence, their admissions of guilt—and the experience had stoked a battle within him, between the desire to get away from these people and the need to stay near them, to communicate the mercy and friendship of a God who had been himself once sentenced to death.

The years of direct contact with execution—the real thing, a life obliterated by the three injections of toxic chemicals into the body—brought about a drastic change in him, to the point where he became a radical opponent of capital punishment. He had been an avid supporter, like his father, and found no alternative in his religious tradition to the death penalty, to the law of retaliation.

Pickett had held one of the victims of the Carrasco escape in his arms. Derisively, Pickett told me, "My whole life I fought for life and for dignity and became a chaplain of death, yes, a 'chaplain of death' and nothing else."

We can scrutinize the death penalty in terms of statistics, crimes, costs, numbers. But we can only truly understand it by seeing its effects on actual people.

—◦—

After graduating from college, Jim Willett started working in the Texas penitentiary system while looking for another opportunity—as many do in Huntsville, and across America, a country where "prison guard" is a professional category similar to "teacher" or "physician's assistant."

Over time, he stopped looking for another job, because he liked the one he had. He worked as an investigator in the internal affairs department of the Texas penitentiary system. Sometimes he felt, sharply, the resentment of his colleagues when he questioned them about abuses reported by the prisoners.

At the end of a long career he became the director of Huntsville's Walls Unit, the standard-bearer for the whole Texas prison system. There are 225 cells in Walls Unit, as well as a rodeo park, an infirmary, and more. In one corner is the Death House, a group of eight cells where a condemned man is brought to live out his last hours. And then there is the Death Chamber, where, when time and legal appeals run out, the man is killed.

From 1999 to 2002, Willett was the warden who escorted condemned men to the Death Chamber at Walls Unit. Recalling his work there, he doesn't remember just the big events, but little things too, the ways the day of an execution is like every other day: the precision required to tidy up the place after the killing; the need to address the practical problems arising from the death of a prisoner, such as legal fees and funeral arrangements.

He breaks out in a sweat when he tells me about the first time he accompanied a condemned man who was rolled into the Death Chamber on a gurney. He describes the man's nervousness, the needle in the vein, the second needle (the back-up needle, which the executioners don't stop trying to insert even though the condemned man is a drug addict and his veins are a mess). This was a man who would not die. As Willett speaks, it seems as though he is reliving the horror when it became evident that death was not coming. Yes, he still sweats when he tells how he had to stop everything and start over. While he speaks, a feeling somewhere between shame and anguish rises to the surface. You can almost can see him giving the order to close the curtain that covers the glass between the death chamber and the witnesses—and then how that time the curtain fell crookedly so that it didn't cover the glass completely.

Jim Willett tells me, "My feelings about the death penalty are very mixed. But I guess it kind of goes to the basics that we shouldn't be killing each other and, once [we do], it messes up the whole chain of what should be happening. I think it's terrible that we have people who commit such crimes that we, as a people in this state, have had to say, 'If you do that, we're going to consider putting you to death.'

"Oh, I've wished many times that we could stop the death penalty, that something would happen to change things, so that we didn't have it anymore. We've got a lot of prisons in Texas. There's over a hundred prisons in our state. If you could get rid of drugs in Texas, you could close down two-thirds of those prisons, I guarantee you.

"I saw a waste of life in many of the executions. The thinking was that this person wasted somebody else's life that may have been very productive. But on the other hand, some of these fellows that are put to death seem to have a good mind, some of them have a good personality, some of them could have been very productive in society.

"So you see the waste of the person who is fixing to be put to death, and then you got the other people, sometimes, that are over there watching these things such as the inmate's family. I mean, they become victims, too.

"Well, society has to have the right to govern, not to say that means they don't ever govern wrong. But those types of questions, I don't have an answer for. I don't know. I have struggled with those questions for years now.

"On the day of executions, after everything was made ready and the inmate was brought in and strapped down, I'd dismiss the officers to go back into the cell block. I would go over behind the inmate's head to a door going into the room where the executioner was, and there were some medical people there and I would tell them that it's OK to come on in and start the IVs. They always, I guess out of habit, started on the right arm and I would get over to the left side and try to carry on a conversation with the inmate, to try to keep him at ease as much as possible and to keep his mind off of what was going on with the needle. When they finished that one, we all just swapped sides. If there was a conversation going on, I would continue it.

"I would just wear these glasses and when it came time,

when the inmate had finished his statement and let me know he was through, I would lower those glasses. And then, usually thirty to thirty-five seconds from then, the inmate took his last breath."

—◦—

The 2000 execution of Gary Graham, known as Shaka Sankofa, was one of the toughest ordeals Willett had ever had to face. The execution of this politicized black man, probably innocent, divided America. Outside the Walls, violent clashes broke out between mounted police and anti-death penalty demonstrators who burned the American flag.

It was the twenty-third execution in Texas that year. Graham had pleaded not guilty and insisted on his innocence right up till the end. In his six-minute final statement he called for a moratorium on executions, performing till his last breath the role of leading activists against discrimination and capital punishment: "Malcolm X and Martin Luther King, Jr. stood up for what is just. ... You can kill a revolutionary, but you can't stop a revolution. ..." Willett has never forgotten those words.

—◦—

Rev. Carroll Pickett told me he became a prison chaplain because he wanted to minister to people who were alive— to be the one who accompanied prisoners to the hospital or went along with them to rehabilitation, who stayed close to them as they re-examined their lives. And then the death penalty was reinstated in Texas and he found himself the chaplain to men condemned to die.

He was the son of an old-fashioned Texan who considered the death penalty as natural as the fact that roads get wet when it rains and dry up again when the sun comes out. Growing up, he just assumed that the death penalty was part of life.

He was a young Presbyterian minister when, in July 1974, he became involved in the Carrasco hostage crisis. During an attempted escape from prison the drug lord Fred Gomez Carrasco took hostages, including members of Pickett's own First Presbyterian Church, and held them captive in the prison's library. Rev. Pickett was called upon to comfort the families of the hostages. After eleven days, Carrasco informed the pastor by phone that he was ready for the escape and allowed him to speak with the hostages who had offered to join him in the escape. Two of them—both women from the Presbyterian Church— lucidly foresaw their own deaths in the failed escape attempt. One begged Pickett to go ahead with her daughter's planned wedding; the other calmly dictated her wishes for funeral and burial arrangements. Sure enough, in the escape Carrasco, one of his accomplices and the two women were killed. Another hostage, a priest, was seriously injured.

Pickett told me how awful it was to hold the dead

bodies of his own parishioners in his arms, to know how brutally they had been killed. He told me how his faith and his convictions, including his support for the death penalty, were strengthened. He went so far as to sponsor an event for the drafting of a document calling for more fervent support for the death penalty in Huntsville.

But it is quite another thing to become a chaplain who accompanies prisoners to death row and the death house, who has direct contact with the convicts, who participates as a moral and spiritual aide within the mechanism that delivers death. It changes you. Helping to care for a man during the last seconds of life, a man who is supposed to be a monster, something to be eliminated, sparks an irreversible change.

Pickett realized that it just wasn't possible that men in good conscience could take the life of other men in such a brutal fashion. He tells of all the counseling he got from a spiritual guide and a therapist. He decided to stay in the job so he could be close to men condemned to death, at least on the last day when they are transferred into the death house.

We talked at length, walking between the crosses on the green lawn of Byrd Cemetery, where inmates whose bodies were never reclaimed by a family member are buried. Until a few years ago, each burial spot was identified only by a number and a tiny cross. An "X" carved into the small cross by the name or number means "executed." Here is some of Carroll Pickett's story as he told it to me.

"I remember clearly the very first one because nobody

had ever been executed by lethal injection; it was the first one in the world. We had no booklet to go by, no format, no advice, nobody to help us out. So the warden at the time, Jack Pursley, he just called several of us together and said, 'We're going to have an execution.' Well, that just shocked us all. Because we knew there was a death house in one of the corners of the Walls Unit, and I was chaplain for [all the] 2,200 inmates there, but I never thought there was going to be an execution. There hadn't been one since 1964. We had put it out of our minds.

"In my opinion, there were at least 10 or more who were innocent, if we want to talk about that, or who were mentally retarded, who could not aid in their own defense. They had no idea what they were doing in the death house. I would explain to them, 'We're going to do this, this, this, and at midnight you're going to die' and they'd turn around and say, 'OK, when we get through with that, when do I go back out to Ellis?' And I'd spend all day with them, explaining to them, trying to persuade them, 'You're going to die,' but these people were not smart enough or intelligent enough to know they were going to be murdered.

"'Thou shalt not kill,' and I think He means that for everybody. He means that for [the prisoners on death row]. But He means it for the state, too.

"We're people. I realize some are bad or evil and they need punishment, but the punishment ought not to be 'an eye for an eye and a tooth for a tooth,' because so many, we are finding now, are innocent. I mean, Illinois has found out [there were too many wrongly convicted men on death row and stopped the executions there]. Over 100 have been released from death rows in America that were innocent. And as the great William Blackstone wrote in 1765, 'It is better that ten guilty persons escape than that one innocent suffer.' We executed innocent people in Texas. I don't care what the governors say. I know they were innocent. And we're going to find out more and more of those, I know, that are lying here in this cemetery, [people who] did not commit the crime. People who can't afford good lawyers—the minorities, the poor, the uneducated, people who happened to be in the wrong place at the wrong time, and again it's mainly people who just can't hire the lawyers to carry them all the way through the process.

"We are all victims of the death penalty. We are paying for the death penalty. We are paying millions of dollars for every big case that goes through. Counties are going broke. The biggest victims are naturally the ones who are [lawlessly] killed, but the man who gets executed is also a victim. Every member of his family is a victim, just as the family members of the one who was murdered are victims. There are many innocent victims.

"They call this the Texas Department of Criminal Justice. Those are contradictory words. Criminal means one thing. Justice means something else. There are a lot of people who need to be in prison. There are a lot of people who have done a lot of bad things, but their punishment shouldn't be something that takes everything away from them.

"When a man who was being executed was through with his final words, final statements that I had practiced with him, he might say to me, 'these are my last words I'm going to say.' So I would nod to him [to indicate that] his speech was over. Then the warden would take off his glasses. There was a two-way window to where the medical people were and as soon as he took off his glasses he would put 'em back on, slide his coat up, and look at his watch. And they would start the execution, they would start the first drug.

"And [the warden] could not see the drug [enter the prisoner's body]. The tube went through a hole in the wall, from the execution room into the person's arm. And so he would tell me to watch and see how long it took. We were working together. He was the legal part and I was his eyes."

—◦—

There is an almost surreal calm in the cemetery. From a distance you can hear the rumble of a tractor or electric mower and see the white jumpsuits of the prisoners tending to the grass or preparing for new burials. Yet it is a peaceful place—a place of pain and suffering where you think about what matters in life.

I have read the letters of death row inmates who didn't

ask for money, food, writing paper, cigarettes, or even a typewriter. Rather, they asked to be permitted to pay for their headstones, so their names could be on their graves: "*I would like to become a human being again, with a name, my name. I don't want to be buried like a dog. Even some dogs have their names at their graves.*"

At the top of the hill inside the cemetery, which is not walled in, there is a huge tomb dedicated to an Indian chief who is buried here. The chief was accused of killing seven settlers in 1871 during the massacre of Salt Creek. He was tried and convicted and sentenced to death. Then his sentence was commuted to life imprisonment. But in 1878 he took his own life here, unable to bear the realities of prison.

—◦—

The Prison Museum is nearby. To a European, the idea of creating a museum out of a jail is absurd. In Dublin there is an entire prison that is a museum, but it is a museum because it was there that the movement for independence from Britain started and developed: up to the 1920s it was where all the leaders of the insurrection and resistance to British "occupation" were imprisoned. A visit to the jail, then, is also a visit to Irish history, a visit to the birth of the nation, a way to pay homage to the founding fathers and heroes of independence. To visit Mandela's Robben Island prison is to visit the history of the new South Africa.

But this prison museum is different. It's a monument to Texas's quest to be a "law and order" state, one that each year invests less and less in its education system and more and more in its prison system. Jim Willett is proud of the fact that nearly twenty-five thousand people visit the museum every year. Many come to see the electric chair, given a place of honor on the far end of the museum. It sits directly in front of the death penalty display window where the three vials used in lethal injections are on display, next to some pictures: a color portrait of the executed Christian *cause célèbre* Karla Faye Tucker, the first woman to be executed in Texas in a century; a photograph of Gary Graham; a brief explanation of the execution procedure, and the remnants of an American flag that the New Black Panthers set afire during the clashes that broke out at the Graham execution.

Next to the stories of prisoners and photographs of the prison as it used to be, there are objects: rudimentary weapons created in jail out of forks and pieces of wood; chains and other implements, such as weighted balls that are chained to prisoners' feet; arts and crafts created by prisoners; and an enormous collection of the various weapons used by prison officials during the long history of the Texas prison system.

Prison City: Life with Capital Punishment in Huntsville, Texas is a book by Ruth Massingill and Ardyth Broadrick Sohn. Its pages are thick with details of what it means to be a guard in the Texas prison system, including the stress that goes with being a part of the Texas Department of Criminal Justice. The authors report that in 2004 one correctional officer out of five in the Texas Department of Criminal Justice quit the job. Likewise, 20 percent—5,511—of the correctional officers directly involved in jobs inside the jails asked to be relieved and had to be replaced.

"Turnover is a big problem," said one of those who left the job. "You get tired of having urine thrown in your face and not being able to do anything about it."

The conditions of life in prison vary, but it is clear that television is considered a luxury on death row. To defend itself against the accusation that the prisons in Huntsville and elsewhere are state-run lounges operating with the taxpayers' money, the prison system has made even television an unattainable comfort.

Many prisons are run by subcontractors, private businesses meant to turn a profit like any other business does. Despite the fact that almost all studies show that rehabilitation and education programs in prison radically reduce recidivism, public opinion is still largely against using taxpayer dollars to educate prisoners. Higher education is offered, but only at the prisoner's own expense.

An examination of the trends in the death penalty in the United States shows that Texas's emergence as the leader is relatively recent. In the years immediately after the Supreme Court reinstated the death penalty in 1976, the states of Virginia, New Mexico, Georgia, and North Carolina surpassed Texas in the number of executions.

The situation changed drastically with the advent of execution by lethal injection in 1982. The single cell that in the past in Huntsville had been used as the death chamber became the death house, with eight cells. This is the place where condemned men spend their last hours before being brought to the execution chamber. From 1982 to January 1, 2013, death row inmates awaiting execution in Texas have numbered three hundred.

When it comes to executions, truly, the Lone Star State stands alone. As of December 31, 2014, 1,430 people have been executed in the United States since the death penalty was reinstated in 1976. Of those executions, 518 took place in Texas, and around 110 each in Virginia and Oklahoma. A second tier of states that have executed more than 50 people since 1976 consists of the Southern states of Florida, Missouri, Alabama, and Georgia. In the last four years alone, there have been twenty-one executions in Florida, thirteen in Missouri, twelve in Alabama, and nine in Georgia. Texas has executed fifty-one people.

The death house is still the death house.

It is striking to see how a single cell, first expanded into eight cells, has today become a whole prison, transferred to another place (the Polunsky Unit in Livingston)—and even now there is not enough space. That the death house has to keep growing shows how ineffective the death penalty is as a deterrent; it also shows that deterrence cannot be the real aim of the frequent use of the death penalty in Texas.

The press kit prepared for journalists covering executions is assembled by the TCDJ officer in charge of media relations—Larry Fitzgerald when I first became involved into the anti-death penalty movement, and now his successor Michelle Lyons.[66] The kit for the media always features the same material, readily adaptable to the new executee: a two-tabbed folder containing a page with figures on executions; a short account of the crime committed by the man about to be executed; the executee's request for his last meal; a list of the coming executions; and a death watch—a summary of the last three days, a sort of deadpan "minute by minute" account of the inmate's last hours.

The death watch (quoted here from *Prison City*) for Douglas A. Roberts, prisoner number 999218, who was executed on April 20, 2005, for a robbery and murder committed in 1996, is typical.[67] In places where the electric chair was used, the pre-execution ritual called for the presence of a special commission to make sure that the head and other parts of the body were shaved properly, in the right places, so that the electrical contact would do the job without setting hairs on fire. The ritual called for a cycle of bursts of electricity starting with 2,300 volts at 9.5 amperes for eight seconds, then a second spark of 1,000 volts at an intensity of four amperes for twenty-two seconds, and then another discharge of 2,300 volts for eight seconds.

Once the cycle of three discharges was completed, the

supervisor had to confirm that the power had been turned off. The contacts were removed and the manual circuit around the chair was disengaged. The security switch was turned on and note was taken of the exact time, minute, that the lever of execution was released. Two minutes after the electric current stopped circulating, a doctor examined the executed body to check for vital signs.

The electric chair, as opposed to lethal injection, did not require the presence of medical personnel during the execution process. But it is always a medic who pronounces the condemned man's death and the time it occurred. (In execution by electrocution, an average of ten minutes would go by from the moment the prisoner was secured to the electric chair to the moment he was pronounced dead.) The doctor signs the death certificate and with an assistant ensures that the documents are properly registered.

If the prisoner is not pronounced dead—a pale bureaucratic euphemism for the situation where a prisoner has been locked into a chair and subject to ten minutes of usually lethal electrical current—then the execution cycle starts again from the beginning. When death is eventually declared, the governor will be notified on a special phone line kept open for that purpose. Next comes a second announcement, to the official witnesses and the media that have followed the execution through a glass window, who are then escorted out of the room and seen off.

In Texas, this ritual has been followed more than five

hundred times. But one doesn't feel that this enormous apparatus of retribution has left the state, or the world, any better off.

4.
Sant'Egidio and the Birth of an
International Movement

1968 was a year of student movements in Paris, Germany, the United States, and Rome.

That was the atmosphere in which I joined what would become the Community of Sant'Egidio, but at the time was just a group of students meeting at a picturesque old Baroque church in the center of Rome: the Chiesa Nuova. When I joined them they had recently started a school for poor children on the outskirts, or *periferia*, of the city, where they had gained firsthand experience of urban violence and the problems it creates. Here were immigrant families living in shantytowns, their children filling the city's jails and correctional facilities. Here were women who had had to put up with the violence of husbands and bosses on a daily basis. For middle-class teenagers it was shocking, but also life-changing: the beginning of a journey that, for many of us, has continued through the present day.

After we were given the keys to an abandoned church and convent in Trastevere—the working-class district of

Rome whose name is derived from the Latin for "across the Tiber"—we took on the name of the church and became the Community of Sant'Egidio. Our namesake (in English, St. Giles) turned out to be the ideal patron: a monk and abbot of the undivided church of the first millennium, he was a follower of the Gospel rather than of any ideology, and a protector of the poor.

We also made it our mission to protect the poor, taking our cue from the Second Vatican Council and Pope John XXIII's message that the Catholic Church "wishes to be the Church of all, and especially the Church of the poor." As time went on, it became clear to us that our mission would involve combating violence, which was how we came to join the fight against the death penalty.

—◦—

Of course, the second half of the twentieth century was a time of violence not just in the suburbs of Rome but all around the world. We heard about the brutality of prisons worldwide, about rulers who used the death penalty against political opponents, about child soldiers involved in an endless war in North Uganda, and so on. The pervasiveness of this violence drove us to the conclusion that capital punishment—as a symbol of the involvement of the State in a process of death, in the destruction of human life—must be overcome.

The Community of Sant'Egidio got involved in the

fight against the death penalty in the 1990s, when the movement was gaining traction, but slowly—fewer than twenty countries had renounced the death penalty in 1975, compared to nearly fifty just twenty years later. And at the time opposition was deeply—if unofficially—split between the pro-moratorium and the pro-abolition fronts, as was apparent to me at the conference in San Francisco in 2000. This division was a problem that needed to be solved. Back in Italy, we sought to introduce some new ideas.

We identified four key problems in the fight against the death penalty:

1. The strategic and operational divide between activists calling for a moratorium on capital punishment (seeking to reduce the practice to a minimum) and those calling for abolition (the outlawing of the death penalty altogether). The latter tended to see the former's strategy as a betrayal, an indirect legitimization of capital punishment; the former saw the latter as impractical, inflexible.

2. The substantial absence of any national or international coordination between anti-death penalty movements in different communities. Each was focused on its own case or region, often in competition with the others, and this reduced the effectiveness of their actions with

respect to both their individual cases and to the broader cause of opposition to the death penalty.

3. The lack of coordination between those movements and public and institutional actions in other countries: local NGOs, for example, were not working or communicating with their own governments, even in countries such as Germany and Denmark where legislative efforts were already well advanced.

4. The challenge of fighting a single issue in many countries with many different systems of governments, laws, and political and social histories.

All these problems had a common root: the conviction that one's own cause is different from everyone else's.

—◦—

In 1998 the Community of Sant'Egidio launched an appeal for a Universal Moratorium Against the Death Penalty. We drafted a text and submitted it to religious leaders we knew through our annual interfaith World Prayer for Peace, as well as political figures and secular opinion leaders. Then we presented it to ordinary people, passing out fliers, speaking at universities, and so on. We started in Rome, then expanded our efforts to the rest of Italy, some other European capitals, and finally the rest of the world. In two years, we collected three million signatures from 145 countries.

On December 18, 2000, we presented the first 3.2 million signatures to UN Secretary General Kofi Annan in his office. The delegation, which I led, included Sister Helen Prejean and Paul Hoffman from the American branch of Amnesty International. Secretary General Annan was deeply sympathetic. We organized a press conference with Susan Sarandon and Tim Robbins at the UN, and later held a demonstration across the street. It was a very cold day, but worth it. Sister Helen, Susan Sarandon, and I met with some people from the abolitionist side. It was then that some abolitionists asked me, "What does it take to collect three million signatures?" I told them, "It takes at least a pencil and a lot of work—and the right cause."

―◇―

"Cities for Life, Cities against the Death Penalty"—a moral, inter-religious, and secular campaign against capital punishment—grew out of the night we lit up the Coliseum to celebrate the end of the death penalty in Albania. The Coliseum, we decided, would be the campaign's symbol, and Rome its driving force. The date chosen for its founding November 30, 2000—was the 214th anniversary of the first official abolishment of the death penalty by a state: the Grand Duchy of Tuscany in 1786.

The aim of Cities for Life was to mobilize civil society

against the death penalty, starting with cities, which in recent decades have become the home of more than half of the world's population. Cities for Life made direct contact, city by city, country by country, with governors, parliamentarians, jurists, law enforcement officers, moral leaders, and other officials, which in many cases expedited the legislative process of abolishing the death penalty, particularly in Africa and Asia. The Community's international network proved useful to grassroots leaders and organizations active in the defense of human rights. Working together, they were able to create national and regional coalitions, and to coordinate more effectively with their counterparts in Europe, Asia, and the Americas.

Chile's repudiation of the death penalty in the wake of General Pinochet's killing campaign was one of Cities for Life's first major successes. Working alongside the Chilean embassy in Rome and the journalist Marcia Scantlebury, who had been incarcerated and tortured by the Pinochet regime, Cities for Life helped to accelerate the legislative process and weaken substantial parliamentary opposition. The moment for a vote came in April 2001, and the death penalty was abolished. We lit up the Coliseum in the presence of Chilean Justice Minister José Antonio Gomez and the Chilean ambassador to Italy.

The event was a dress rehearsal for the first Cities for Life Day on November 30, 2002. Approximately eighty cities participated that first year, and since then the number has steadily increased, reaching 1,600 in 2013.

Participating cities illuminate a monument—such as the Coliseum—to commemorate the first state to abolish the death penalty, to promote events, and to show their commitment to life.

The French NGO Together Against the Death Penalty (*Ensemble contre la peine de mort*, or ECPM) was another group working hard to abolish capital punishment. ECPM promoted the first World Congress Against the Death Penalty in Strasbourg in 2001. Twenty-six representatives of as many international associations, including the Community of Sant'Egidio, signed the Strasbourg Declaration on June 22, 2001, committing to "create a worldwide coordination of abolitionist associations and campaigners, whose first goal will be to launch a worldwide day for the universal abolition of the death penalty." On May 13, 2002, they founded the World Coalition Against the Death Penalty in Rome, at the Community of Sant'Egidio's headquarters in Trastevere. An executive committee of eleven associations and NGOs became the movement's strategic nerve-center. Since its founding, the World Coalition has worked to abolish the death penalty by lobbying organizations and states and supporting local activists. The World Day Against the Death Penalty, held for the first time on October 10, 2003, is another important part of their strategy: together with Cities for Life Day, it has become an annual flashpoint for global mobilization against the death penalty.

―◯―

Sant'Egidio had had enormous success in mobilizing in Europe, but, as we knew all too well, the fight against the death penalty is an international one. Thus, we turned our attention to the United States, which has a long history of using capital punishment. First, we worked to tighten relations with many American groups against the death penalty, such as Journey of Hope, the Texas Coalition Against the Death Penalty, and Murder Victims' Families for Reconciliation.[68] All this coordination not only helped to make US movements less isolated, but also boosted European mobilization at a time when the question of judicial error was gaining a foothold in mainstream conversation: a growing number of prisoners were being released because they had been either proven innocent or shown to be victims of glaring legal discrimination.

Sant'Egidio also got involved with the defense of John Paul Penry, the intellectually disabled convict whose death sentence was overturned three times. Over the years, the Supreme Court had declared the execution of the intellectually disabled unconstitutional, but their ruling did not stop the state of Texas from trying to convict Penry a fourth time.

In the Penry case, humanitarian activities and diplomacy promoted a standard of moral decency hard to ignore in a globalized world. The campaign to save Penry, which involved disability rights organizations, finally succeeded when the US District Court for the District of Eastern Texas decided to commute Penry's death penalty to life in prison with no possibility of reprieve, a solution that his legal team accepted. As of January 15, 2008, John Paul Penry was no longer on death row. And Penry's case was successful in more than ways than one: it also encouraged American organizations to take part in the international gatherings, facilitating Sant'Egidio's efforts to merge all groups into a single movement against the death penalty.

—◦—

Things weren't just happening in the United States. In its humanitarian work, Sant'Egidio came into contact—through letters and legal efforts—with areas generally ignored by European activists, particularly in Asia and Africa. Through the years, Sant'Egidio has launched direct initiatives and urgent actions to halt executions in ninety international cases—for instance, the case of Safiya Hussaini.

On October 9, 2001, Safiya Hussaini Tungar Tudu was charged with adultery and sentenced to death by stoning in Nigeria. She was pregnant at the time. The Community's website published the first online petition on behalf of Safiya's plight, and it was picked up by major international news organizations, particularly the Italian and British media.

On November 27, 2001, more than twenty Italian senators heeded the Community's appeal and urged Renato Ruggiero, Silvio Berlusconi's foreign minister, to appeal to the Nigerian government to save the woman's life. Sant'Egidio sent a letter to Nigerian President Olusegun Obasanjo requesting that the "inhuman sentence" not be carried out. Even though Safiya's case was formally a matter for local government and so out of the central government's hands, the letter represented an important step that prompted substantial involvement on the part of the Italian government in the cause to save Safiya's life. On December 18, another sixty parliamentarians signed on to the official request to the Nigerian government. Meanwhile, demonstrations were organized in Italy with the help of a popular radio station and the attention of the media in general.

On International Women's Day, March 8, 2002, the Council of Europe launched an appeal on behalf of Safiya and Nigerian women in Italy, who faced the danger of expulsion and repatriation to a country that punishes prostitution and adultery with death. On March 17 there was a silent vigil in front of the Nigerian embassy in Rome following a statement from President Obasanjo in which he said he was "hopeful" that there might be a favorable outcome.

It took six months of international mobilization, but five days later, Safiya was acquitted and became a free woman again.

Sant'Egidio succeeded in this case because it gained public support through news campaigns, international mobilizations, joint actions with other groups, and the involvement of parliamentarians and diplomats. Publicity campaigns are not usually a part of Sant'Egidio's strategy, but they may become necessary when basic human rights, such as the right to a defense, or the right to life itself, are at risk.

—◦—

It was in this context of humanitarian activities, carried out through direct diplomatic contacts with political leaders, that the death sentences against two Lebanese citizens in the Democratic Republic of the Congo, Sami Yassine and Khalil Ghodban, were annulled. Laurent Kabila, president at the time, granted the Community's appeal for a pardon in this and in other, lesser-known cases.

In Cameroon, the death sentences of two young men held in the prison of Tcholliré were commuted after the Community got involved with the legal work and contacted local authorities. At the same time, the Community sponsored an international campaign on behalf of prisoners, taking on the battle for the liberation of inmates with definitive death sentences, whose appeals had been exhausted. In many judicial systems, executions do not take place automatically, and even without legal defense they can be annulled in exchange for financial compensation or by official act. Thanks to the Community's efforts, as an example of the kind of actions that over the years have become global, the death sentences of fourteen other prisoners were commuted between 2003 and 2004.

The Community's interventions have not always worked. In Morocco, we tried without success to save Merzoug Hamel, an Algerian sentenced to death for a massacre he did not end up participating in—abandoned by his accomplices, he had fired his clip into a wall. The death sentence remained in effect despite the efforts of the Community and the light shed on the case by Mario Giro's book about it, *Gli occhi di un bambino ebreo* (*The Eyes of a Jewish Child*), which was translated into several languages. Morocco has since joined the list of countries that appear to be respecting a *de facto* moratorium.

In Central Asia, the persisting influence of state socialism on judicial institutions, and the habitual lack of transparency in the relationship between citizens and central power, combine to create a dangerous situation. The fundamental rights of legal defense are frequently denied, and the death penalty is used as a weapon against political opposition.

The Community of Sant'Egidio began the Central Asia branch of its mission in Uzbekistan, where the government kept the burial place of executed prisoners secret, making it impossible to ascertain whether prisoners had been physically tortured before being put to death. Working with an extraordinary woman, Tamara Chikunova, and her association "Mothers against the Death Penalty and Torture," the Community succeeded in averting the executions of twenty-two prisoners. We also succeeded in securing new trials and subsequent acquittals for five death row prisoners. Another five death row candidates were proven innocent before the sentence was handed down. This success was brought about through our involvement with the legal process and civil affairs, at great personal risk, which required the backing of an international movement to defend the lives of those exposed to the most extreme danger—first and foremost, Tamara Chikunova herself. Deprived of her freedom, her safety threatened, she received aid on numerous occasions from the Italian, German, and French embassies in Tashkent, through the good offices of the Community. The effort to obtain complete abolition took about seven years to complete, but on January 1, 2008, the Uzbek government revoked the death penalty for all crimes.

The road to abolition was marked by fewer obstacles in Kyrgyzstan. The capital, Bishkek, was the first city of Central Asia to join the Cities for Life movement. On June 27, 2007, the law to amend the Criminal Code was enacted, replacing the death penalty with life imprisonment. The new law also provided for a review of past capital punishment trials. And on January 1, 2008, Uzbekistan was the first state in the world to abolish the death penalty after the approval of the UN Resolution at the General Assembly.

The Supreme Court of Kyrgyzstan had six months to review all of the death penalty cases commuted to life imprisonment. According to Article 384 of the Criminal Procedure Code, the sentence handed down by a judge can be revoked and the trial can be reopened if there is new evidence to bring to the case.

In March 2007, the Community of Sant'Egidio undertook a mission to Kazakhstan in order to probe the possibility of getting the government to adhere to the moratorium on the death penalty under discussion by the UN. Kazakhstan gave a favorable vote to the Resolution in December 2008. The mission was preceded by talks with the Italian Minister Plenipotentiary and head of the European office of the Italian Foreign Ministry Laura Mirachian, and was organized in close coordination with the Italian Ambassador in Kazakhstan, Bruno Antonio Pasquino. It was a successful case of combined institutional action.

During the visit, Community representatives had talks with several of the country's civil and religious authorities. On the opening day of the conference, Pope Benedict XVI met with the participating religious leaders in the presence of the Ecumenical Patriarch of Constantinople, Bartholomew I; the primate of the Anglican Church, Rowan Williams; and the chief rabbi of Israel, Yona Metzger. The talks touched upon several political and religious issues, with an emphasis on the international moratorium on the death penalty and inter-religious dialogue.

The Community of Sant'Egidio made an official

request for a moratorium on executions by law and offered its legislative assistance. Kazakhstan's first response to the Community's request, drawn up in conjunction with the Italian Embassy, was to agree to sign the preliminary protocol of intent for an initiative at the UN launched by the Italian foreign minister.

Then in October 2007, in Naples, the president of the Kazakh Senate announced that he was going to introduce a legal moratorium on executions. In the days that followed, the Kazakh parliament formally ratified a moratorium on executions. Shortly thereafter, the death penalty was abolished for ordinary crimes in Kazakhstan.

—◦—

At the end of the 1990s, President Abdurrahman Wahid of Indonesia, home to the largest Muslim population in the world, was no doubt the most influential Muslim figure to sign the UN's appeal for a universal moratorium on capital punishment. His signature paved the way for a series of debates and reflections, which the Community of Sant'Egidio aided through direct contacts with the Indonesian authorities. The contacts continued through the crisis surrounding the 2006 execution of three Christians accused of playing a key role in a revolt that claimed many lives. The Community promoted and coordinated an international campaign to save the prisoners' lives and downgrade the charges against them.

International efforts did not stop their execution, but the movement of parliamentarians in favor of a moratorium by law gained ground.[69]

Meanwhile, a debate was raging between the Justice Minister, the Supreme Court, and the executive powers about the commutation of seven thousand death sentences in Pakistan. On October 30, 2006, and in August 2008, the Community of Sant'Egidio negotiated pardons from the victims' families for three death row inmates, blocking their executions. From 2008 to 2012, Pakistan observed an unofficial moratorium, but it ended with the execution of Muhammed Hussain, a soldier convicted of murder, on November 15, 2012.

By then, the moratorium in Indonesia had led to a special protocol of agreement and collaboration between Sant'Egidio and the largest Indonesian Muslim organization, the Muhammadiya, one that constitutes a huge step forward by opening this organization to the abolition of the death penalty.

Sant'Egidio had more success in sub-Saharan Africa, where in the space of just a few years the number of abolitionist countries had grown from four to fifteen. Aside from numerous contacts with officials from death penalty countries, from 2005 to 2008, the Community of Sant'Egidio, which had a network of local members spread throughout the region, organized a series of international conferences in Rome attended by twenty-five African Justice Ministers, who took part in public forums, workshops, and closed-door sessions. The presence of political and judicial officials along with representatives of Sant'Egidio paved the way for a series of processes mobilizing legal aid and support for legislative proceedings, thus establishing a new and more effective venue than the traditional recourse to petitions and appeals.

—o—

Since 2003, the World Cities for Life Day events, held in conjunction with the Tuscan regional administration and the City of Rome, have represented the most widespread international mobilization against capital punishment. Since 2006, the European Union has recognized and supported the Community of Sant'Egidio's project for the creation of an international network that would support human rights organizations and spontaneous groups of citizens against the death penalty in retentionist countries, especially in key geographic areas. One of the goals: to foster the birth of regional coalitions and the empowerment of local activists and humane civil societies. Collaboration with the European Union has greatly factored into the Community's success: if this link were to be weakened it would limit support for decisive regions, such as the Caribbean and the Middle East.

In 2008, the UN held discussions on how to proceed with a new resolution in the General Assembly, a year after approving the first resolution. The debate between European countries and the cosponsors of the previous resolution focused on the advisability of presenting a "strong (political) resolution" or a more "technical" one. They opted for a "hybrid" text, which introduced some new concepts, such as the need for information and transparency, while incorporating the recommendations of Secretary General Ban Ki-moon's first report, published in September.

The Resolution gained more supporters, 104 in all, and fewer opponents, forty-eight. The matter was put off until the Secretary General's next report and a new resolution would be presented. Meanwhile it was agreed that the issue would be examined on a biannual, rather than annual, basis. The mood had changed.

While there was a setback in Liberia—which reinstated capital punishment in 2008, violating its earlier adoption of the UN resolution—things were looking up in the United States. Just before the first UN Resolution in 2007, Governor Corzine of New Jersey signed a bill of abolition. New Mexico followed suit in 2009, and a few days later, the 131st innocent prisoner was released from death row in the United States. On April 16 of that year, Colorado had an abolitionist draft law approved by one of the two houses of the legislature. In April 2014, New Hampshire, the only state in New England where the penalty remains law, considered a repeal bill, which received a tie of twelve for and twelve against, and remains, for now, before the state senate. New York, Illinois, Connecticut, and Maryland have also abolished capital punishment. It's not enough—but the story isn't over yet.

5.
Timeline: From Death to Life

The current turn against the death penalty is something truly profound—as epochal a change in the twenty-first century as the turn against slavery in the nineteenth, or the turn against child labor in the twentieth. The times they are a-changin'—and it seems possible that capital punishment, like slavery and child labor, will eventually be consigned to history.

⟞⟝

3100 BC: In ancient Egypt, the death penalty is the punishment for crimes against the state. Convicted criminals are executed by impalement.

1760 BC: In the Code of Hammurabi, the death penalty is invoked for twenty-five different crimes, including adultery and helping a slave to escape; murder is not one of them.

Sixth century BC: The Book of Exodus, probably written

during the Babylonian captivity, records the *lex talionis* (Exodus 21):

> 23 *And if any mischief follow, then thou shalt give life for life,*
>
> 24 *Eye for eye, tooth for tooth, hand for hand, foot for foot,*
>
> 25 *Burning for burning, wound for wound, stripe for stripe.*
>
> 26 *And if a man smite the eye of his servant, or the eye of his maid, that it perish; he shall let him go free for his eye's sake.*
>
> 27 *And if he smite out his manservant's tooth, or his maidservant's tooth; he shall let him go free for his tooth's sake.*

458 BC: Aeschylus depicts the death penalty as a form of vengeance in the *Oresteia*. But Orestes is a reluctant killer: his mother, Clytemnestra, has killed his father, her husband, Agamemnon, so Orestes feels obligated to avenge his father by killing her. In his reluctance, we see the beginning of the humanist refusal to pursue the death penalty as a form of revenge.

428–348 BC: In ancient Greece, Plato argues that there must be proportionality between the crime and the punishment the Republic metes out. He sees the death penalty as a way for the polis to educate society and deter future crimes, and recommends capital punishment for intentional homicide, theft, obstruction of justice, and treason, among other crimes.

Fifth century–First century BC: Roman methods of execution: Beheading, beating, burning, animal attack, burying alive (in the special case of the Vestal Virgins who had broken their vows to celibacy), and crucifixion.

73 BC: Spartacus leads a slave revolt against the Roman Empire; six thousand captured slaves are crucified along the Appian Way from Rome to Capua.

50 AD: Under Nero's persecution, Christians are fatally impaled at the Coliseum.

339–342: Constantine's nephew Flavius Claudius Julianus (Julian the Apostate) receives a Christian education from Eusebius of Nicomedia; as emperor, he will forbid Christians to serve in the military, as they are unwilling to inflict death.

Fifth century: Hanging is introduced as a method of execution in Anglo-Saxon Britain.

747: In Tang dynasty China, Emperor Xuanzong abolishes the death penalty, replacing it with scourging or exile, depending on the severity of the crime. Abolition lasts only twelve years.

818–1156: Under the influence of Chinese culture, which he admires, and allied with some Buddhist schools, Japanese Emperor Saga, who is said to have introduced tea drinking in Japan, abolishes the death penalty. Abolition lasts more than two centuries—the longest abolition ever to that point in history. In fact, some ninety years earlier, in 724, at the start of the reign of Emperor Shomo, the death penalty had been abolished, but only for a few years.

1351: In Britain, the Treason Act defines high treason and petty treason in law; high treason is a capital crime, punishable by death.

1533: "The vice of buggerie," or sodomy, is made a capital crime in Britain.

Circa 1540: Under Henry VIII, there are eleven capital crimes, including high treason, petty treason, rape, piracy, arson, and murder.

1542: Witchcraft is declared a felony punishable by death in Britain.

1608: First recorded execution (for treason) in the British American colonies takes place.

1671: In Britain, the Coventry Act makes it a capital crime to intentionally maim or wound another.

1682: Pennsylvania limits crimes punishable by death to treason and murder.

1699: Shoplifting to the value of five shillings or more is deemed a capital crime in Britain.

1718: In Britain, the Transportation Act allows the courts to sentence convicted criminals to be "transported" to America for seven years.

1764: Italian jurist Cesare Beccaria, age twenty-six, publishes *Dei delitti e delle Pene* (*On Crimes and Punishments),* the first major European legal text to call for the abolition of the death penalty. "It seems absurd to me," says Beccaria, " that the laws . . . which execrate and punish homicide, should themselves commit one, and that to deter citizens from murder they should order a public murder."

1786: Tuscany becomes the first modern state to abolish the death penalty and torture on November 30.

1787: The newly framed United States Constitution provides for the death penalty in both the Fifth and Eighth Amendments. Founding Father Benjamin Rush (who has read Beccaria) opposes this.

1789: In Britain, Catherine Murphy, alias Bowman,

convicted of high treason, is burned at the stake, the last such execution in the UK.

1791: The first bill to abolish the death penalty is presented in France on May 30.

1791: The French penal code, which provides for execution by guillotine, is formally adopted on October 6.

1795: The death penalty is abolished in France for a single day—a day of general peace on October 26, at the revolution's end.

1810: Napoleon reinstates the death penalty in France on February 12.

1820: the last execution by hanging followed by decapitation is performed in Britain on May 1.

1822: William Reading is hanged for shoplifting, the last time that crime is so punished in Britain.

1830: Venezuela, under Simón Bolívar, becomes an independent state and ceases performing executions.

1833–1835: In the US, public executions, declared overly cruel, are replaced by private hangings in many states.

1832–1837: In Britain, Sir Robert Peel's government introduces various bills to reduce the number of capital crimes. Shoplifting, as well as sheep-, cattle-, and horse-stealing are removed from the capital crimes list in 1832, followed by several other crimes in the next five years.

1835: In the last executions in Britain for sodomy, James Pratt and John Smith are hanged at Newgate.

1837: In Britain, Old Bailey judges are empowered to commute death sentences for crimes other than murder.

1843: Rev. George Barrel Cheever and anti-slavery crusader John O'Sullivan lead debates against the death penalty in New York.

1845: The first national death penalty abolition society, the American Society for the Abolition of Capital Punishment, is founded in the US.

1846: Michigan becomes the first US state to abolish the death penalty for all crimes except treason.

1848: San Marino, a tiny independent state within Italy, bans the death penalty for civil crimes.

1852: Rhode Island becomes the first US state to abolish the death penalty for all crimes, including treason.

1863: Venezuela bans the death penalty for all crimes.

1868: Great Britain outlaws public hanging, requiring executions to be performed behind prison walls.

1877: Costa Rica bans the death penalty for all crimes.

1887–1903: Thomas Edison demonstrates the power of electricity by electrocuting animals.

1890: In New York, convicted murderer William Kemmler becomes the first person to be executed by electrocution on August 6.

1908: Great Britain outlaws the execution of children under the age of sixteen.

1924: The US's first gas chamber is installed in Nevada, on the idea that death by asphyxiation is more humane than by hanging, firing squad, or electrocution.

1933: Great Britain prohibits the death sentence for persons who were under eighteen when they committed their crimes.

1936: On August 14, Rainey Bethea is hanged in Owensboro, Kentucky, before a crowd of twenty thousand people—the last person in the US to be executed in public.

1939: Eugen Weidmann is executed by guillotine, the last public execution in France; the event was captured on film. It can be seen today on YouTube.

1946: On January 4, Theodore Schurch becomes the last person in Britain hanged for offenses under the Treachery Act of 1940.

1948: The British House of Commons votes to suspend capital punishment for five years; the House of Lords overturns the decision.

1949–1953: The Royal Commission on Capital Punishment is convened in London.

1953: Julius and Ethel Rosenberg are executed in the electric chair at Sing Sing prison in upstate New York, the first US civilians to be convicted and put to death for espionage.

1957: British Parliament passes the Homicide Act, limiting the death penalty to five categories of murder.

1960: Anthony Miller is the last teenager to be hanged in the UK. He is nineteen years old.

1965: Capital punishment for murder is abolished in the United Kingdom; treason, piracy with violence, and arson in Royal Dockyards remain capital crimes.

1966: Wong Kai-Kei is the last person to be put to death in Hong Kong. When Hong Kong is incorporated in the People's Republic of China, it declines to restore the death penalty, which is in widespread use in China.

1969: On December 18, Parliament confirms the abolition of capital punishment for murder.

1972: The US Supreme Court rules 5–4 in *Furman v. Georgia* that the death penalty is unconstitutional as administered in the United States, overturning six hundred cases and instituting a *de facto* moratorium on executions. All five justices concur in the judgment that the death penalty is applied unfairly and arbitrarily in the US. Two of the justices, William Brennan and Thurgood Marshall, declare the death penalty unconstitutional in any form.

1974: In the US, the National Conference of Catholic Bishops publicly opposes the death penalty.

1976: The US Supreme Court, in *Gregg v. Georgia*, reaffirms the constitutionality of the death penalty on the grounds that state executions, if properly conducted, do not constitute a form of the "cruel and unusual punishment" prohibited by the Eighth Amendment.

1977: Gary Gilmore is executed by firing squad in Utah on January 17, the first person to be executed in the US in almost ten years. The *de facto* moratorium on capital punishment ends.

1980: The American Medical Association starts to discourage participation of physicians in executions on the grounds that doctors' "powers are dedicated to the preservation of human life, not to the service of death."

1982: The first execution by lethal injection is carried out in Huntsville, Texas, on December 2.

1987: Michel Radelet and Hugo Bedau publish a groundbreaking study in the *Stanford Law Review,* documenting 350 cases of persons convicted for capital crimes in the United States between 1900 and 1985 who were later found to be innocent.

1993: Kirk Bloodsworth, on death row in Maryland, is released from prison after being exonerated through DNA testing—the first such exoneration.

1995: Djibouti, Mauritius, South Africa, and Spain abolish the death penalty for all crimes.

1996: In Delaware on January 25, Bill Bailey is the last person executed by hanging in the US.

1996: Belgium abolishes the death penalty for all crimes.

1996: John Martin Scripps, in Singapore, is the last Briton to be hanged for murder.

1997: Nepal and Poland abolish the death penalty for all crimes; Bolivia abolishes the death penalty for ordinary crimes.

1998: Armenia, Azerbaijan, Bosnia and Herzegovina, Bulgaria, Estonia, Lithuania, and the United Kingdom abolish the death penalty for all crimes.

1999: Turkmenistan abolishes the death penalty for all crimes. Latvia abolishes it for ordinary crimes.

1999: German national Walter LaGrand is executed in a state gas chamber in Arizona, the last person to be put to death by asphyxiation in the US.

2000: Ivory Coast, Malta, and Ukraine abolish the death penalty for all crimes.

2001: Greece abolishes the death penalty for all crimes. Chile abolishes it for ordinary crimes.

2002: Cyprus, Serbia, and East Timor abolish the death penalty for all crimes.

2002: By a 6–3 majority, the US Supreme Court

rules the execution of intellectually disabled offenders unconstitutional.

2004: Bhutan, Samoa, Senegal, and Turkey abolish the death penalty for all crimes.

2005: Death sentences for offenders younger than eighteen are ruled unconstitutional under the Eighth Amendment.

2005: Mexico and Moldova abolish the death penalty in all cases.

2006: In China, the Supreme People's Court affirms that capital sentences imposed by regional and local courts must be reviewed by the Supreme Court. This policy reduces executions in China by nearly 30 percent.

2006: Georgia, Montenegro, and the Philippines abolish the death penalty for all crimes.

2007: Albania, Kyrgyzstan, and Rwanda abolish the death penalty for all crimes.

2007: New Jersey abolishes the death penalty, the first US state to do so by legislative action since capital punishment's reinstatement as constitutional in 1976.

2007: On December 18, the United Nations General Assembly passes a resolution calling for a universal moratorium on the death penalty.

2008: China replaces the firing squad with lethal injection as its chief method of execution.

2008: Uzbekistan abolishes the death penalty for all crimes.

2008: In New York State the moratorium against executions established by law in 2004 becomes a definitive ban on the death penalty, and the state's death row is dismantled.

2009: The death penalty is abolished in New Mexico.

2009: On December 8, Ohio becomes the first state to perform executions using a single drug, sodium thiopental.

2011: In Illinois, the state legislature passes a bill calling for the abolition of the death penalty. Two months later, Governor Pat Quinn signs it, making Illinois the sixteenth abolitionist US state.

2011: China removes thirteen economic offenses from its list of capital crimes.

2012: Connecticut becomes the seventeenth US state to abolish the death penalty.

2013: Governor Martin O'Malley, who has backed efforts to repeal the death penalty since their legislative origins, signs the bill that makes Maryland the eighteenth abolitionist state in the US.

2013: Five hundredth recorded execution in Texas.

2014: Washington State Governor Jay Inslee suspends the death penalty.

2014: Tennessee passes a law allowing for execution by electric chair.

2014: On July 16, US federal judge Cormac J. Carney rules that California's death penalty violates the US Constitution.

2014: On October 23, Pope Francis calls for the universal abolition of the death penalty.

2014: On November 21, the Third Committee of the UN General Assembly passes a new resolution calling for a worldwide moratorium on executions, with 114 votes in favor, thirty-six against, and thirty-four abstentions.

6.
Some Thoughts on the Origins and Abolition of the Death Penalty

It was a child who first sought to abolish capital punishment in the West.

Pietro Leopoldo was Grand Duke of Tuscany between 1765 and 1790, and then became the emperor of Austria in his last two years. Modern scholars call the penal code he established the Codice Leopoldino, or *Leopoldina*. While it may be seen as a child of previous codes, it establishes many new interpretations. On November 30, 1786, in Florence, the city of Dante, Leonardo da Vinci, and Michelangelo, the death penalty was abolished and torture was outlawed for the first time.

To get here—to Archbishop Desmond Tutu saying "to take a life when a life has been lost is revenge, not justice," and to Pope Benedict XVI welcoming the ministers of justice attending the "No Justice Without Life" conference to a private audience and urging them "to do all that is possible to abolish the death penalty"—has taken longer than twenty centuries. Why?

—◁◦▷—

Reaching back some 3,500 years before the *Leopoldina*, the Code of Hammurabi, from the eighteenth century BC, provides some answers. It was the first document codifying the death penalty. In it, capital punishment is prescribed as the punishment for twenty-five different crimes—not only for homicides but also for crimes against property. In other words, it codifies the idea that the punishment can properly exceed the crime. The punishment was widely disproportionate—to kill someone, for example, as punishment for the crime of theft—but at least for the first time an attempt had been made to implement an orderly system of rules, with legal sanctions to punish crime.

In ancient Athens, Draco introduced severe punishments for different crimes, an approach that gave rise to the word "draconian," and that in our own times might be called "zero tolerance." The settling of personal quarrels and family feuds generally involved murder or the threat of murder. When Solon published new laws, Draco's homicide statutes were kept as valid.

The ancient Roman legal system is the basis for the legal systems of all Western countries, and for the West's application of the death penalty in particular. The Roman Code, devised largely by Salvius Iulianus and, later on, deeply influenced by Gaius in the second century AD, came about six hundred years after the so-called Twelve

Tables (450 BC), which codified crimes and punishments in writing so as to prevent abuses by the patricians and aristocrats, who might otherwise use criminal accusations to suppress revolts by the citizenry.

Public treason was the crime that most especially was punished by death, but a host of more private crimes could lead to death, too. Crimes against property, fraud in changing the borders of one's land, lying, cheating a client, stealing during the night, infringing a promise, or violating a woman—all these could be punished by death.

It's worth taking a few sentences to list all the different ways the death sentences were carried out in "the old days," since people in modern times have hardly altered them. Beheading, drowning, cutting off the condemned person's limbs; putting the victim in a bag and dumping the bag in a body of water, sometimes including snakes or bees in the bag; hanging, flogging, burying alive (in the case of the Vestals, whose blood could not be dispersed), or throwing the convict from a high place (as was often done to slaves who had stolen from their masters), impalement, and, for non-Romans, crucifixion (as in the case of the Revolt of Spartacus).

The Pentateuch, the first five books of the Hebrew Bible, maintains that the death penalty is to be inflicted in the case of murder, violation of the Sabbath, blasphemy, and a wide range of sexual crimes, in addition to magic rites. Although actual executions were very rare, because of the difficulty of producing eyewitnesses to the act of adultery, the death penalty was a natural part of the society that produced the Bible. But it is possible to trace the practice's evolutionary development from immeasurable revenge ("seventy times seven") to proportional punishment ("an eye for an eye, a tooth for a tooth"), to a way of thinking (found in the Book of Job) that entrusts the power over human life to God alone, not to human society or worldly justice. The New Testament goes further, and indicates the path to ending violence is the path of forgiveness in every circumstance, even in the face of a wrong inflicted; central to this path is the rejection of death as a punishment, as made emphatic by the execution of Jesus, who was sentenced to die by the vast and imperfect justice system of the Roman Empire but whose crucifixion accomplished absolutely nothing in a worldly sense, only in a spiritual one.

Early Christians were persecuted by the Roman Empire for their beliefs. For example, in the third and fourth centuries, a wave of repression, forced conversion, and violence called the Diocletianic Persecution swept across the Roman Empire, leading to the arrest, torture, and murder of much of the church hierarchy. These executions were sometimes made into public spectacles, with Christians being tied to posts and fed to lions in the arena. Emperor Julian the Apostate declared Christians "bad citizens," ineligible for military service on account of their non-violent attitude. But with the ascension to the throne of Emperor Constantine later that century, there came a ruling that it was unlawful to execute Christians, much less to use them in public spectacles or let them be slaughtered by the lions.

—◦—

Although it is true that in Islam capital punishment has been accepted from the beginning and has during certain historical periods been popular, it is also true that the tradition of turning away from capital punishment has its own long tradition. While the Caliphs in Baghdad during the Abbasid period implemented terrible punishments, Islamic nations on the whole have preferred mercy to killing, and sharia law entertains the possibility of private settlement between a murderer and the family of a victim, allowing them an opportunity to spare the killer's life, with or without financial compensation.

In China, capital punishment was common from the tenth century to the beginning of the twentieth, and a common form of execution during much of that time was the *lingchi*, or slow slicing—"death by a thousand cuts." But capital punishment was banned between 747 and 759, the time of the Tang dynasty, at the behest of Emperor Xuanzong. Criminals sentenced to death were now scourged with a rod or exiled to the Lingnan (the end of the world) instead—something close to the Greek idea of "ostracism," the banning an individual from return to country and society. This change in policy did not last long, however. When the Lushan Rebellion rose up and threatened the unity of the empire, the death penalty was re-introduced. It was used rarely, however—only a few dozen times during Xuanzong's reign, which lasted for forty-four years.

In Japan capital punishment was abolished by Emperor Shomo, briefly, in the eighth century, and then as soon again as 818, by Emperor Saga, under the influence of Chinese culture and Buddhist schools. This time, the ban lasted for more than three centuries, until 1156. Just a little later, in Italy, St. Thomas Aquinas supported the doctrine of the need to accept a "minor evil" to gain a "major good." It was centuries after St. Augustine had defined the concept of "just war."

In Europe, the most significant statement against the death penalty came nearly three centuries later, in the Twelve Conclusions of the Lollards, a manifesto written by followers of John Wycliffe and posted on the doors of St. Paul's Cathedral and Westminster Abbey (the message boards of the time).

In the eighteenth century, Voltaire made a utilitarian case against the death penalty, arguing that it was useless because it produced no "profit" to society. A generation later, Jeremy Bentham also saw capital punishment as a net negative, since it reduced the plenitude one of society's main sources of wealth—namely, human beings.

Earlier, Thomas Hobbes's approach had been to somehow create an exception to the idea of the social contract only for the death penalty. In society, Hobbes saw individuals acting on the basis of a natural instinct to make a contract to create the maximum advantage for each individual and for all together. But capital punishment did not fit this scheme—because how can the person sentenced to death reckon it an advantage to be killed? So Hobbes made an exception to his own contractualist philosophy and justified capital punishment as a legitimate form of retribution on other grounds. According to David Heyd, a scholar in ethics and bioethics at the Hebrew University of Jerusalem, this is due to Hobbes's tendency to see human nature as fixed and inclined towards bad behavior.

The nineteenth-century Italian anthropologist Cesare Lombroso, the founder of positivist criminology and author of *L'Uomo Delinquente*, or *Criminal Man*, also saw some humans as genetically inclined towards evil, and thus accepted capital punishment as a natural solution. He also thought he had demonstrated once and forever a connection between physical defects and wild or savage behavior. This was only a few decades before the "new scientists" in Germany would develop theories of Jewish behavior based on physical traits such as curly hair, sharp cheekbones, and long noses.

—◦—

The founders of the US (like the leaders of the new independent countries of Africa two centuries later) adopted the criminal codes of their former rulers, Great Britain. As early as 1612 in the American colonies, killing chickens owned by others, stealing grapes owned by others, and trading with Indians were all crimes punishable by death. Somehow the European Enlightenment arrived in America without the initial energy and imagination that in Europe had led to innovative approaches to the death penalty. Strangely, the Enlightenment had led to the abolition of the death penalty in Tuscany, and also, for a short time, in Catherine the Great's Russia, but not in America.

Surely John Calvin, the spiritual inspiration of many of the first European inhabitants of New England, was not so extreme to suppose that some people were "predestined to die" at the hands of the state. Nevertheless, his influence is recognizable in the process that led the civil authorities to place the responsibility for poverty and for crimes arising from poverty squarely on the people who committed them, without any mitigating factors. In England, crimes against property were punished relatively mildly, while punishment for "immoral" crimes such as rape were published harshly. In any case, at the end of the nineteenth century in America there were 220 crimes punishable by death through the "bloody code."

The "bloody code" first appeared as the criminal justice model in pre-modern England. Somehow, the judge had to define the perfect candidates for exemplary executions, choosing from among the many people who had committed the same crime and who, according to the law, were deserving of the ultimate punishment—choosing those who could best become deterring examples. As Norma Landau of the University of California writes early in her monumental study *Law, Crime, and English Society, 1660–1830*, the main goal of the English trial and judicial system was "deterrence." The idea was that most defendants would receive detention as a minimum punishment, while a few "exemplary" criminals would be executed as a deterrent. But a strange thing happened: more criminals received the death penalty than ever before, and executions became free public events attended for amusement by thousands of onlookers.

In America's antebellum South, another level of crimes was created—crimes by enslaved blacks against whites—and a list of punishments was created to deal with them. A "bloody code" was elaborated for crimes committed by slaves and other blacks, one without any counterpart in the "white justice" system of the time.

The US Bill of Rights, influenced by the writings of Italian philosopher Cesare Beccaria and ratified in 1791, had served to limit death sentences by prohibiting the state's use of "cruel and unusual punishment" in its Eighth Amendment. Some scholars today argue the term "cruel and unusual punishment" was a standard verbal formula, understood differently by the framers than it might be today. Nevertheless it was a formula that started to limit the use of the death penalty to the harshest cases—presaging, perhaps, language in the Constitution of India, drafted much later, that says that death sentences must be contemplated "in the rarest of the rarest cases." Yes, what is "cruel and unusual punishment" is under dispute, but this reflects the fact that times are changing, and with them the standards of decency considered acceptable by the different communities and—now—by the western and globalized world.

The brutalities of slavery brought with them a renewed interest in capital punishment, which led in turn to still more brutalities. They also stimulated the abolition movement in the United States, which in the middle of the nineteenth century became one of the most powerful social movements America had ever seen. Cesare Beccaria, to whom we owe the beginning of the abolitionist process in the Western world, observed how "the last entreaty never dissuaded the men determined to wipe out the blight of offences to society." In his *Dei Delitti e delle Pene (On Crimes and Punishments)* he went even further. He asserted that the certainty of a conviction is a more effective deterrent than the seriousness of the penalty. In a text published in 1776, he declared that, because of the social contract, no citizen can yield the right to dispose of his personal life, concluding that "the death penalty is not a right, but a war of an entire nation, which deems necessary the destruction of a human being, against a single individual. This does not enhance society."

—<o>—

America's current approach to capital punishment carries within it all the different threads of its past: The British penal code, the harshness of Calvinism, the brutalities of slavery, and a shining history of successful social movements that includes the abolition movement as well as the pacifist, worker's rights, and civil rights movements. So the story in America is not a simple one. There is remarkable change and there have been major steps taken in America to overcome our addiction to the death penalty. And at the same time, America is far behind other countries on this important journey.

Today in America, the argument to justify the death penalty as a form of deterrence, or as a form of retributive justice, is often set against the utilitarian argument that a judicial system based on the death penalty costs more than it is worth. And it is true that the costs of administering the death penalty are truly appalling. It is surreal to think that in California there are 745 death row inmates and that the state Supreme Court of California devotes fully one-third of its work to capital cases, even though the "productivity" of the system (if it can be called that) is as low as one execution every three years. Appalling and surreal. But in the last quarter of the twentieth century social attitudes toward the death penalty began to change dramatically.

In the 1970s, the number of abolitionist countries in Europe started to grow, partly as a result of efforts there by Amnesty International, and informed also by the memory of the senseless killings of two world wars, as though Europe were finally proclaiming, "Enough with death!" after the millions of killings on their soil. Outside Europe—with some exceptions—economic growth and the demise of some authoritarian regimes, as well as globalization, encouraged opposition to the death penalty. In the United States, meanwhile, the Supreme Court, after a short pause in executions, once again gave the green light to capital punishment in 1976. When executions resumed, Texas emerged at the forefront: since the resumption, Texas alone has progressively accounted for about 30 to 50 percent all the executions in the US (even though California has the larger death row), with lethal injection being the principal method, thanks to the claim that it's painless and so avoids "cruel and unusual punishment." Lately, this claim has been challenged by the scientific community and professional associations.

Michigan was the first US state to abrogate the death penalty in 1847. Since then, another seventeen states and the District of Columbia have followed suit, while the death penalty remains on the books (with varying degrees of application) in the rest of the country. Meanwhile, to give you an idea how this compares with some of our closest allies, Great Britain entered the ranks of abolitionist countries in 1971, Canada in 1976, France in 1981, and Australia in 1985.

Mongolia is the most recent Asian state to have abolished the death penalty, through a process initiated by its president, Tsakhiagiin Elbegdorj, in consultation with the Community of Sant'Egidio and Amnesty International. In the twenty-first century, the trend toward abolition has spread to Africa and Central Asia. As of October 2014, eighty-one countries have ratified the Second Optional Protocol to the International Covenant on Civil and Political Rights: Latvia, Mongolia, Guinea-Bissau, Poland, and El Salvador, most recently. And 167 states are party to it in one way or another. Over the last six years, fifteen states have ratified it (Chile, Argentina, Honduras, Rwanda, Uzbekistan in 2008, Brazil and Nicaragua in 2009, Kyrgyzstan in 2010, Benin and Mongolia in 2012, Bolivia, Guinea-Bissau, and Latvia in 2013, Poland and El Salvador in 2014).

That is real progress. Even so, it will be some time before we reach ratification by one hundred countries—the target Amnesty International set in our discussions in the late nineties before it would take the Resolution for a Moratorium to the UN General Assembly. It may take another twenty years. Meanwhile, the Second Optional Protocol is the only binding international document that represents the clear, official, international disavowal of the death penalty, even though it allows for a resumption in the case of war.

—◦—

Albert Camus, writing out of his experience in French Algeria, assaulted the death penalty with passion and eloquence. More and more, his view is becoming that of the majority:

"[B]eheading is not simply death. It is just as different, in essence, from the privation of life as a concentration camp is from prison. It is a murder, to be sure, and one that arithmetically pays for the murder committed. But it adds to death a rule, a public premeditation known to the future victim, an organization, in short, which is in itself a source of moral sufferings more terrible than death. Hence there is no equivalence. Many laws consider a premeditated crime more serious than a crime of pure violence. But what then is capital punishment but the most premeditated of murders, to which no criminal's deed, however calculated it may be, can be compared? For there to be equivalence, the death penalty would have to punish a criminal who had warned his victim of the date at which he would inflict a horrible death on him and who, from that moment onward, confined him at his mercy for months. Such a monster is not encountered in private life."

7.
Voices in the Silence

"No sandals, no visible toes, no tank tops."
—Rules for death row visitors

The unspoken aim of death row is to break the wills of the prisoners and to emphasize the idea of their inhumanity. In that way, when the day of the execution arrives, it will seem that the person whose life is taken is in a sense not really a human being. But against all odds, Dominique Green has grown up in here. He's become a man. He writes poetry, he paints. His art expresses anguish. There's a rose, emerging from a man's eyes, with tears that drip from the thorns and travel far, like a letter sent from prison. There are small spaces, intertwined bodies, grilles and bars everywhere. The death chamber stretches out, its shape like a crucifix.

John Paul Penry has grown here, too, and learned how to read a little, even if it is clear that he will never be a grown-up in any of the ways we understand that word to have meaning. When I met him, the US Supreme Court had annulled his sentence twice, saying the lower courts did not take his disability into account, but each time the state of Texas has had the last word and he is still on death row.

Eddie Johnson used to call himself "the Warrior" in his letters. He was under eighteen when he was arrested, and eventually ended up here on death row. He's always been at war with the system, fighting a losing battle.

--o--

Dominique Green had become pen pals with Stefania Caterina and a couple of my friends, Luis and Barbara, living in Rome. Stefania, a clever, sensitive woman living near the Vatican, is a member of the Community of Sant'Egidio. It was thanks to her and Dominique Green that we all entered death row for the first time.

After several years of letters back and forth with Dominique Green, I wanted to meet him in person, which meant traveling to death row in the Polunsky Unit in West Livingston. I wrote several letters to the administration and thought I had been placed on the visitors list. I booked my flight and hotel room and went to Texas. After I arrived, I was told that I did not yet have permission to visit and that it was not clear whether I would be granted permission in time. But it turns out that there are special, more lenient, rules for members of the media. A way in was available to me after all, so long as I entered as a journalist.

It turns out there's one day a week when members of

the media are allowed to enter death row, so long as the inmates and their lawyers agree. It is one of the contradictions of the American penal system. It is a closed system, a total institution that is not governed by the same rules and ideals that apply in the world outside. Nevertheless, there is some transparency, and in keeping with the idea of an evolved democracy, the media have easy access. This access can be understood in two ways. In one, a mature democracy should have nothing to hide and death row should be no exception, so it is positive that the media can penetrate prisons. But there is also a different way of seeing the situation—as yet another flagrant example of the unequal power among human beings, where members of the media have special rights while friends of the condemned have no rights at all.

So I filled out the media request form and asked my assistant at RAI, the Italian public television network, to send, as required, an official request from the office in Rome. I contacted RAI's New York bureau and got the contact details for some TV production partners in Texas. In Houston, I hired a two-person TV crew at my own expense, for a rate of one thousand dollars per day, and on the scheduled day the three of us entered the prison. The State of Texas was playing with me; I was going to play, too.

I had no intention of making a film. All I wanted was to meet Dominique Green, John Paul Penry, and Eddie Johnson, friends of mine. But since I had the crew with me, I started to film. I was not conducting interviews, I was filming life on death row, talking to my friends while my friends were talking to me. To be precise, life was flowing and the camera was just recording. Death row is all about extremes: either no life or lots of life.

The meeting room where we were is painted white and has a bulletproof glass wall down the middle. There are seats for visitors on one side of the glass wall and cubicles for the inmates on the other. Visitors speak to inmates on an old black phone.

Beyond the meeting room, behind the sturdy walls, armored doors, and bullet-proof glass are three hundred convicts in white jumpsuits emblazoned with the letters DR, constantly reminding them of their appointment in Samarra.

Dominique Green

"As far as violence, that's one thing you have to throw away, because it's something you cannot succumb to in here. Because you have no [way to] win. If you do anything the repercussions are so drastic, you lose. So it makes no sense to act that way. If anything, try to outthink the oppressors. Since you know [that's what] they're trying to do to you, don't give them a reason to do something to you."

John Paul Penry

"I remember the first time I came here. That was back in 1980, the exact day was March 9, 1980. Yeah. It seems like a big old dream to me that has never come true. You know... a big old nightmare for me. You know, come to find out—one of the guys said, 'Johnny, you need to wake up and face reality [as it really] is.' I said, 'I am.' He said, 'No, you're not.'"

Eddie Johnson

"I [had] completed eight years of school. I was still in [high] school when I came here.... Being here on death row has matured me and educated me a lot. But I wish I could have continued studying."

John Paul Penry

"There's another inmate who taught me how to read the Bible. John 3:16. 'God so loved the world that he gave his only begotten son.' I read that scripture. He quoted [it to] me over and over again, and told me that I'm doing good. He said now that was a test. This here is a real test. So he told me pick up a pen, or a pencil and a piece of paper and he taught me how to write my letters. You know, like, 'Dear So-and-so, How are you doing? My name is Johnny Penry.' That's how I started my letters out. Told of how long I've been on death row. My first letter, I got a response."

Dominique Green

"I forgave my mother a long time ago. You know, she put me through a lot coming up. I hated her for a while. But, you know, that was before I understood and I really took the time to look at the life she had. And doing that I realized that she was just continuing the cycle. Her mother went through things and passed it on to her and she went through things, and tried to pass it down to me. But I didn't pass it on. I was the person who broke the cycle. Unfortunately, I wasn't able to break it quick enough, and I found myself here.

"But I broke it. Because I raised two little boys, my two little brothers and so far they got me, you know, with their success, to the point that I did good. From how I grew up, being in this position now, I would say that growing up the way I did, being in a cycle of violence, it prepared me for a situation like this, even though it wasn't supposed to happen like this. So I can adjust to it, and not let this place wear on and get the best of me, because I've been mentally prepared a long time, though I didn't know it. You know, it's funny how everything works itself out, but that's what happens."

Eddie Johnson

"They segregate us into levels: Level 1, Level 2, Level 3. Level 1's are regular, they get to have radios, typewriters, and appliances and go to the commissary. And have a visit once a week. Level 2's aren't allowed to have any appliances at all. They take our t-shirts, socks even, and underwear, right? And they give us what they call state. State attire and it's pretty much just thrown-together. It's two thousand, twenty-five hundred people and everybody's got to share it like. Most of us elect not to wear them at all, but they only let us buy hygiene [products] on Level 2, and stamps. That's all. And only two visits a month. On Level 3, we can't buy nothing at all. And we aren't allowed to have no deodorant, no toothpaste, nothing, man. All we can buy is postage, that's all."

Dominique Green

"We come with a whole other approach of how we handle the system. We don't throw piss or shit on them, or stuff like that. We go through the processes of the grievances. Try to work things out, and if we have to, we file lawsuits. Which is something other prisoners don't think about because they're conditioned into reacting. And they don't get the way we act. Whereas we're taught to be more patient, more understanding. To think more about how to make things happen. Because in reality, if you send us to die, well, I mean it just puts so much of your life in perspective. It makes you look at things in a whole other way. Where you just want to be who they want you to become or who they want you to be."

Eddie Johnson

"I talk to the dudes that are, like, in the next cubicle from mine. We can't see each other, but we can hear each other. We talk sometimes about a lot of our experiences in the world, our experiences here. Just a lot of different things, we compare thoughts and opinions, ideas. All that stuff."

Dominique Green

"You know, we debate. We argue, we do everything to just pass the [time] and at the same time to keep our humanity, right?"

Eddie Johnson

"Signing my letters 'Sir Eddie' [instead of 'Eddie the Warrior'] means that I know now I am not an animal. I don't have to express it like that. I've matured to the point where it doesn't matter what they think. Because I know in myself that I am not an animal, right? And that I'm a human being just like everybody else. I use 'Sir' with my name, because that's how I feel. I feel worthy of life. You know what I'm saying? The kind of respect that every human being's got."

John Paul Penry

"I remember when I had a date and it was a real scary one. I came within three hours of being executed and that's about the closest I ever got. So far, I've had four dates and the fourth one, it got real, real scary. And I smoked me some cigarettes, drank me some tea and I was still, my head was still messed up over that. Right now it's still messed up. I can't help but think about it."

Dominique Green

"When a society will stoop to lawlessness to, I guess, eradicate lawlessness, basically what you're saying is you're going to become killers to kill killers. And to do that, you throw all the rules out the window. So innocent people, retarded people, mentally impaired people—all of them gonna get caught up in that wheel because lawlessness doesn't care. I mean, it's all about exacting revenge and so that's what always makes the death penalty wrong: the fact that to enforce it there are things you have to do away with. There can be no fairness. You have to break the rules to get what you want, to murder people. That's the thing about a killer. When somebody wants to kill someone, do you think they're thinking about how to do it fairly? It doesn't make sense, trying to kill somebody fairly."

Eddie Johnson

"By the same laws, the people who made capital punishment legal commit murder, commit capital murder also. So the dude who injects the fluids in our veins, he commits murder under their laws. So, it's not justifiable at all because they're saying it's all right for him to kill us, but it's not all right for somebody else who's not a part of their group to kill somebody. So it's just a big contradiction."

Dominique Green

"How many people here in death row are innocent? You know, I've done legal work and I do any legal work for any prisoner who asks me for it. I've come to believe that it's between 10 and 30 percent.

"I've seen so many cases that are just rife with errors and the attorneys didn't do nothing, the investigators didn't do nothing. The police were rushing to solve the case. And it's not like [the accused] had any money to fight. So they weren't no different than me. It's just that in their case what you look for—the only thing that could probably save them—is the number of errors that were made. That's all it comes down to.

"I think the last poem I wrote was maybe one month ago. I've recently started helping other prisoners that are trying to write poetry and stuff like that, so I'm more like an editor now. I show them how to compose poems, create stanzas, and all this. I'll walk them through the poetry process, because one thing poetry initially did, it made me want to write more. Poetry opened the door for me to write articles and stories, so I use it as a vehicle to teach other people how to write. It starts off with poetry, but slowly it evolves to something else.

"Each time, it costs like $2.5 to $7 million to execute one of us. There are 320 capital cases in process right now. I was going to show that with those numbers you just spent between one and seven billion dollars to kill 320 people. I mean, you could take that money—the price that they are paying to kill me—and invest it in my life. I could have a beautiful future. But they don't invest in our lives. Instead, they invest in destroying."

—◦—

At 7:59 PM on October 26, 2004, Dominique Green dies by lethal injection. He is the 331st convicted murderer to be executed in Texas—and the 938th convicted murderer to be executed in the United States—since 1976. His last words are, "There was a lot of people that got me to this point and I can't thank them all. But thank you for your love and support. They have allowed me to do a lot more than I could have on my own . . . I have overcame a lot. I am not angry but I am disappointed that I was denied justice. But I am happy that I was afforded you all as family and friends. I love you all. Please just keep the struggle going . . . I am just sorry and I am not as strong as I thought I was going to be. But I guess it only hurts for a little while. You are all my family. Please keep my memory alive."

The coroner writes on his death certificate, "Cause of death: Homicide."

Dominique Green

"Since I got here, it's just trying to defy the system and get out, if that can be. Just—I don't know, man—that's the only thing I guess that really pushes me to accept these days and carry on the struggle: the fact that I could be fighting for all the chips or I could be fighting for nothing. The only way I will find out is to keep fighting."

8.
Curtis McCarty—A Friend *Off* Death Row

In 1982, a young woman named Pamela Willis, a drug user and the daughter of a local police officer, was killed in Oklahoma City, Oklahoma. Her naked body was found showing signs that she had been sexually assaulted, stabbed, and strangled. In 1985, Curtis McCarthy, a twenty-two-year-old man who had been interviewed and released shortly after the crime, was arrested for the murder. On the basis of testimony that his hair matched hair found at the crime scene, McCarthy, who had known Willis, was convicted and sentenced to death.

In the year 2000, attorneys for McCarthy, following the discovery that a police chemist had falsified forensics results in other cases, pressed for McCarthy's case to be reopened. After seven years of effort—including comparisons of his DNA with DNA obtained from sperm and flesh found on the victim's body—McCarthy was exonerated. In order to link him to the crime police officials had given false testimony. On May 11, 2007, he was freed, after twenty-two years in prison, nineteen of them on death row. He was the 201st convict to be proven innocent through DNA testing, and the fifteenth who had been sentenced to death.

I sat with McCarthy in 2008—he was forty-four—and asked him about his experiences.

He spoke slowly and combed his beard while talking.

Can you describe a normal day on death row?

The prison imposed no routine so we made our own routine. We would eat breakfast, have coffee, and read or study until lunch. And then in the afternoons we would exercise, try to stay healthy. In the evenings, we'd watch television or play cards or read more. There really wasn't anything else to do, you know. Write letters to our families.

Can you describe the cell to someone who has never seen it?

Death row was at a facility called the Oklahoma State Penitentiary at McAlister, Oklahoma. The "Big Mac." When I first got there in 1986, we were in a classic old sand block kind of building with lots of steel bars and no hallways, but then they decided to build the H Unit: concrete and solid steel doors. They built it underground and that's where I was housed from 1991 until I was freed. H Unit is one of the new super-max prisons they are building across America, where they completely isolate the inmates from each other and from the staff so that you cannot have human contact.

The cells were very small: Eight steps that way and eight steps this way, because out of boredom we walked— eight steps one way, eight steps back. There was no natural light. There was no proper ventilation.

It was a terrible place to be. They would bring breakfast about 7 AM, lunch around noon, dinner at 4 or 5 PM. That was about the only routine we had with the staff, the only thing that occurred in our lives that was regular. Many men used that as their clock: breakfast came, so it was time to get up, to read and exercise or whatever.

Why is it underground?

They told the public, through the media, that it had to be underground because the death row inmates were dangerous and the guards were fearful. But that wasn't true. It seemed they designed the building to be as cruel as possible, as inhumane as possible. And when it was built, they threw a party. They let their politicians, their supporters, their founders come there and spend the night and they had live music and food and they celebrated that monstrosity. We had very little property—books, pencils, and paper—but still the public and the politicians thought we were being treated too well.

What is life like without ever seeing natural light? How did you know when it was night and when it was day?

What they called the exercise yard was actually inside the building: a very tiny space where they would put four or five men at a time just to stand there and talk to each other. They cut a hole in the roof so light would come in. You could look outside your door—there was a large window in the door—and you could see out to the yard, So there was light coming down, you could see that, but there was no light coming into the cells. So we could see if the sun was up or down, but you couldn't see the sky or the moon or the sun.

Was there more noise, or silence?

Death row at night was quiet. During the day most of the staff was there. So many men were awake then, awake and dissatisfied with the way they were being treated.

They would turn their TVs up loud just to aggravate the staff, beat on their toilets just to make noise, just to let the staff know that they were there and they were dissatisfied. But when the administration left in the evening, it would get quiet, so my cell mate and me, we usually stayed up at night most of the time.

You were sentenced to death. You had nothing to do with the murder. How did that make you feel?

When they charged me with murder, I wasn't afraid. I still believed the things that my government told me when

I went to school, that my family told me: that we have an excellent judicial system, that it is honest, and that our Constitution protects us from wrongdoing. How could they punish someone for something they didn't do? I found out the hard way that that's not true: that our system is corrupt, that it's mostly governed by politics, by revenge, that issues of guilt or rehabilitation don't matter. I found out that Politicians are very sensitive to public opinion, to what the newspapers say and to the general call to be tough on crime. And I found out that they can break the law to get good stories about themselves published in the newspapers.

Tell me about your case. What happened? Why were you sentenced to death?

I had a good life when I was a child, and I was enthusiastic about education. But despite that, when I became a teenager, I started taking drugs and I lost sight of all the things that are important to all of us: family and community and spirituality.

By the time I was sixteen, I was no longer in school. I didn't see my family the way I should have, at holidays and birthdays. I began to commit crimes and to go to jail, and I never seemed to learn my lesson. I just kept doing it. My parents didn't know what to do. And it seemed that my community didn't care; they just let me go my way.

When I was twenty years old I met a young woman named Pam Willis. Pam was the daughter of a police officer in Oklahoma City. She too had dropped out of school because of drugs and didn't pursue her education. She wasn't a bad person either, but she made poor choices that had terrible consequences for her, just like I did. I didn't know her well—she was only an acquaintance.

In December of 1982, she was found raped and murdered in her home. Because she was the daughter of a police officer, there was an intense investigation to find the man who had raped and killed her. There was also the embarrassment, because it was an issue of drugs.

So any man who had any kind of acquaintance with her was asked to come to the police station for questioning, and I was one of those young men. So I went to the police, voluntarily, I told them who I was and how I knew her.

They took my statement, they collected physical evidence from me: hair, blood, saliva, fingerprints, palm prints. They took my photos; they gave me a polygraph exam. When they were finished, they told me I was free to go home; they had no more questions for me. They had everything they needed from me plus the evidence gathered at the scene of the crime, which did not correspond. This was why they let me go. I didn't hear from them again for almost three years.

The Federal Police, the FBI, and the Innocence Project all say that I was eliminated from the list of suspects. But some three years later, they said they heard a rumor that I had told somebody that I knew who did it. And that wasn't true. I had only repeated a rumor I heard myself that it must have been her drug connection who had killed her. I had no personal knowledge of the matter; I had just repeated what someone told me.

They resumed the investigation. They realized that I lived an immoral life. They knew that the public wouldn't like me very much. And that that no one would care if I were to be designated as "the murderer."

The second time, they didn't invite me to the police station, they came and took me by force. They grabbed me and shoved me into the car. They lied to all of my friends. They told my friends that I had made statements against them, and that wasn't true. They were trying to break me. While I was at the police station, they hit me, they abused me psychologically and physically. There was nothing I could tell them [to change their attitude to me].

Despite the person I was then, the life I lived of drugs and crime, my heart was still good. I knew what had happened to her was terrible and if I had had any information I would have told them. There was nothing I could say. I had no knowledge. But they didn't care.

At the end of that day, the man who represented the government told me that he thought I was a liar and that if I didn't tell him who killed Pam immediately, I would take that man's place in court.

I didn't have an answer, and he kept his word and charged me with first degree capital murder. And so I stood trial for a crime that I did not commit.

How did they prove your guilt in order to sentence you for first degree murder?

Because there was such a large amount of evidence collected from the crime scene, they had to hide that evidence, which is illegal. Joyce Gilchrist, the chief forensics examiner for the police department in Oklahoma City, took the stand and under oath told the jury that the semen and the hairs found on the victim belonged to me. I was poor. My family didn't have the money to hire the experts I needed to come in and say, "There's something wrong here."

And the jury believed her. They didn't ask, "Why didn't you arrest him three years earlier? Why did you let him go free?" They let me go because it wasn't me; and those twelve men and women who sat in judgment of me didn't consider that.

They convicted me and because of my past misconduct they sentenced me to die.

They heard terrible things about me, some that were true, and some that weren't true. They were told of my supposed involvement in another murder. That wasn't true. I had no way to defend myself; I couldn't invite good friends or community leaders or a priest—I didn't have anybody like that who would come and speak in my name.

What happened inside you when you heard the sentence in the courtroom?

When they came back and they said, "Death," I couldn't believe that my government had betrayed me, but I was resigned to it, that maybe it was better. Even a life sentence is a death sentence, you go to prison and you never come home. Our government tells everyone else in the world that we have an excellent system, that you should use us as a model for your own system. So my heart was already broken; when they came back and said, "Death," it was just a little bit more on top of my suffering.

For the first few years on death row, I raged. I became angrier every day. During the time that I awaited my trial, I had had time to sober up, to reflect, and to realize how terribly I had damaged my own life. And I learned from it. When I got to death row, I began to read. I tried to resume my education, to become informed and to try to start making wise decisions in my life. So I read and I talked to people and I observed. And I especially studied the law and the death penalty. And the more I read and the more I listened, the angrier I became. I saw the men around me, I saw the racial disparity, I saw that every man who was on death row—they were drug addicts, they were poor, they were all uneducated, men who were vulnerable, who society didn't care about. They were disposable human beings. The government would say, "He's a bad man, he did this"—and people would believe them.

I saw that the men on death row weren't monsters, they were human beings. Many of them had mental disabilities. Others had damaged their minds almost beyond repair because of drug abuse and alcohol. There were men who hadn't committed terrible crimes, who had committed homicide, but who didn't *deliberately* kill someone. There were men who had good defenses for what they had done—self-defense—but because they were bad men, the government could say, "He's lying."

There were a number of men who had done terrible things, things that made even me angry for what they had done. Serial killers, who killed and killed and killed. Our government said that those men, especially, needed to die. And I learned that even the serial killers had value to society. One of the men, who was a serial killer—the FBI came and visited him regularly. They examined him. He agreed to cooperate and they got inside his head, trying to figure out who he was and why he had done what he did so that they could see those signs in other kids and set them on a different path.

In your opinion, how many death row inmates are innocent?

There were many men that I met that I think it is fair to say were innocent of murder. Politicians are so obsessed with their own headlines that they make up their own rules. The worst of those rules is called the *Felony Murder Rule* in Oklahoma, and other states they call it the *Law of Accomplices.* They can use that law to convict *everybody* involved in a crime of murder. The best example is the armed robbery where two men go to rob a store and one man stays in the car because he's the get-away driver. The second man goes in the store to get the money from the storeowner and there is a struggle and the proprietor is killed. They will put both men on death row and they will tell the public they are both guilty of murder even though the other man was in the car. He should be punished, but we should remember that he didn't kill anybody.

What was it like when one of your friends was going to be put to death?

The men on death row were my neighbors. Some were dangerous, some were crazy, so you had to have friendships to protect yourself. There was strength in numbers, so you had strong bonds of friendship and concern—love for each other. So I made many friends. They all died. All of them. Anytime one dies you keep dying for a long time.

Did you ever think of committing suicide?

At the beginning, no. As I said, when I first got to death row, I was angry, I was bitter. I had been betrayed by my government and I hated the men and women who committed those crimes against me. After a few years, I realized that I was acting just like those people, acting out of hatred and revenge. It was me now who didn't recognize their humanity or their fallibility. I saw them, I guess, as objects, just like they did me. And it took me a while to mature, to grow up into a man and realize that I couldn't live my life that way with hatred in my heart and always thinking of revenge. That it was unproductive and it was unhealthy. Not just for myself, but for everybody around me.

I realized that I couldn't hate them, because hating them made me like them. Hating them kept me imprisoned—kept me from being free. And I stopped hating those people. And I began to mature, to become a man, to have some wisdom in my life. And it brought me peace.

After some years passed, I received relief from the appellate court—they said I should have a new trial because of misconduct—but I lost again. Years later, I got more relief and I lost again. *I was sentenced to die three times for that crime.* And each time I would lose a bit of hope. Each time they killed one of my friends, I would lose hope.

By the year 2000, it was as if I were already dead. There were many new men coming onto death row, and I tried not to make friends with those guys because I knew what was going to happen: I would hear about their children and see the photographs and hear the stories about them and their families growing up and birthdays and Christmas and their mothers. And then I would have to watch them die.

When I was arrested I had two children. I was not a good father. I was selfish and I was a drug addict and I didn't honor my responsibilities to my children. What should have been a joy for their mother—in raising children—instead became a burden because they had no father. And by the time I gained that maturity to realize that they needed me in their lives, I was already incarcerated and there was nothing that I could do to help them. They were never told where I was. They were simply told that I was a bad person and I had run away. My family thought it was better that they thought of me that way than to think of me sitting on death row.

The most that I could do each night was to think about what I had done that day: The letters that I wrote or the books that I read. Was it a productive day? Did I do something good for myself or for my family? And it would help me sleep at night, so that I could have some pride in myself. But as the years passed, I didn't even do that.

When you go to death row, they tell you to fill out your last will and testament. I never did, because in my heart I knew that someone would eventually see what had happened to me and know that it was wrong.

In January 2001 they killed my friend Billy, and I finally did it: I sat down and filled out my last will and testament. And I wrote goodbye letters to my mother and my father. And I had decided that I wasn't going to let the state kill me, I wasn't going to give them that satisfaction.

Do many people kill themselves on death row?

Some did it with drugs — drug overdoses. Others just

stopped their appeals and told the government: "Just kill me. I'm not going to argue about it anymore. I can't live in these terrible conditions."

Can you tell me what, and from which friends, you learned the most on death row?

I think I learned from them all. First I learned humility—that the world didn't revolve around me, that we were all part of a larger community, and that my selfishness was no good—that I couldn't live my life that way. I learned not to hate the staff. You know, we were often mistreated by the staff, but I didn't hate them. I understood them as human beings. They were fallible, they were victims of a mistaken way of thinking and a bad system; they had their own problems that made them do things they shouldn't have done, just like I did.

I still do things that I should not do. I'm forgetful, I'm late, I forget people's names and I'm rude. I don't mean to be, it happens. I'm fallible. Which was the better way to live my life? To be selfish or to be altruistic?

Did they reimburse you?

No, the government in Oklahoma still does not publicly acknowledge that they did anything wrong. Only one of the people who committed the crimes has been publicly identified—the Gilchrist lady, she lost her job. That's all. The detectives who brought the false case to the district attorney's office have not been identified. The man who told me to my face that he would file a false charge against me is now a judge in Oklahoma County. He sits on the bench and makes judgments in these kinds of matters. He is an immoral man; he shouldn't have that position. One of the two homicide detectives—the one who beat me—is now the chief of police in Oklahoma City.

So who do I go to to say, "They've committed crimes and must be held accountable for what they did?"

In Oklahoma, we have a law for prisoners that says when you leave prison, every man—to at least make sure that he can get home to his family—gets $50 and a bus ticket. They wouldn't even give me that. No apology, no nothing. I think in my maturity, in this little bit of wisdom that I have found for myself, I don't need their acknowledgment. I can live my life without that.

They stole twenty years from your life. Are you angry? Do you hate anyone in particular?

I do not hate. Anyone. If I did I would still be a prisoner. And I would be like them, like the system. To give up hatred is the only way to be free, fully, forever.

What is your dream?

I dream always of justice and fairness. We have enough in the world now: we have enough knowledge; we have enough resources that we could be fair and generous to everybody. We have enough to share with the poor, with the unfortunate, with the disabled. They don't have to live their life the way they do. We have enough to share with them.

I dream about "equal justice under the law." Most of the people who end up in court are guilty; they did it. But you don't have to crush them to teach them a lesson. You don't have to lie to the court or lie to the jury. Treat them honestly. Show them compassion. Show them that revenge is no virtue.

Jesus was sentenced to die. That makes Jesus a brother of anyone on death row.

Yup. Sentenced to die by a corrupt and frightened government that mistreated him, that didn't know how to treat Jesus with respect, to acknowledge his humanity, to sit down and talk to him as a man.

Would you give up the things you learned on death row in exchange for never having been there?

No. It was a horrible thing to have to live that way day after day after day for years and years—the betrayal and all of the death. But I think it brought me wisdom. Because of the way that I led my life, I would have gone to prison for something. I don't mean to minimize what they did—what they did were crimes against humanity—and they didn't do it only to me, they did it to others. They tortured me and tried to kill me and to use me for political purposes—so I didn't learn anything from them. I learned from myself. I learned from my neighbors and my family and from the people who have shown me love and understanding. I wouldn't trade those lessons and that wisdom for anything.

9.
Life Row

All ways of looking at the death penalty turn our eyes to the murder victim's family members. Over the years, I have come to know many such people, including Arthur Laffin, Marietta Jaeger, Renny Cushing, and Bud Welch. To spend time with them is to try to understand the pain and sense of loss they feel; the process of rage, anger, despair, sorrow, and emptiness; the difficulties they find in coming to terms with the absence of the loved one who disappeared so abruptly and unexpectedly; the resignation and the hope of healing. I have learned a lot about life and death from each of these people. And I think there is a treasure of wisdom that we can learn from them, an "art of living" that goes beyond the death penalty, and that concerns life itself and how to live it. This is life row.

—◦—

In 1999, Arthur "Art" Laffin's brother, Paul, was stabbed multiple times by a resident as he was leaving St. Elizabeth's homeless shelter in Hartford, Connecticut, where he had worked for ten years. He died shortly after. The man who killed him, Dennis Souta, was homeless and mentally ill. He would later be found mentally incompetent to stand trial and sentenced to sixty years at a Connecticut prison hospital.

Paul Laffin was killed at the gathering place of a community he believed in and was committed to serving. Now Art continues his work. A longtime organizer, speaker, and writer in faith-based movements for peace, justice, and nonviolence, Art is a member of the Dorothy Day Catholic Worker House in Washington, DC. He has participated in an annual "Starvin' for Justice Fast and Vigil" at the US Supreme Court to call for the abolition of the death penalty; has taken part in the Journey of Hope in North Carolina, Ohio, Texas, and Virginia; he has spoken in Italy during Sant'Egidio's "Cities of Life" campaign. At the end of October 2014, we were both in Manila, where we succeeded in promoting the first Asia Pacific Region Dialogue, "No Justice Without Life," with thousands of young people, officials, and authorities. Later I learned that, as early as 1997, Art was arrested for unfurling a thirty-foot banner across the steps of the US Supreme Court that read "Stop Executions." Art told me why he does what he does:

> My family and I, and all who knew Paul, still grieve his senseless, horrific death. My brother truly gave his life for those he served. What happened to my brother is not uncommon. It

is a societal disgrace that some of the mentally ill homeless, who fall through the cracks and are not properly cared for, end up committing lethal acts.

My family and I were appalled, but could not desire the death of someone who was not capable of dealing with his life. Evil creates sorrow and pain. More pain and more killing does not alleviate sorrow.

After Paul's highly publicized death, my mother and I appealed to the public to show mercy toward Dennis and to pray for him. I also requested that all necessary resources be made available to provide continuing care for Dennis, and all other mentally ill people, so that tragedies like what happened to Paul might be averted in the future. Only forgiveness gives closure. Hatred leaves you alone and prevents any closure.

Every family member of a murder victim ultimately reaches this decision: death row or life row? Art chose life row as the only way to break the cycle of suffering.

―◦―

Marietta Jaeger is "only" a mother, if it is possible to say such a thing. While her family was on vacation, camping in Montana, her seven-year-old daughter Susie was kidnapped from the family's tent. For one year, they knew nothing of Susie's whereabouts. She had disappeared. Marietta felt hope and anguish in turn. Hope is the last emotion to die, but the very persistence of it can increase suffering, since without closure it is impossible to know how to begin grieving, only to hold ones breath and suspend the pain.

On the first anniversary of Susie's disappearance, the kidnapper telephoned Marietta and inadvertently revealed sufficient information to enable the FBI to identify, locate, and arrest him. He, too, was mentally ill. There was evidence that he had killed Susie and three other young people in the same county. As he was arraigned, Marietta asked that he be offered the alternative allowed in capital cases in Montana and other states: that is, a mandatory life sentence without possibility of parole instead of the death penalty. The prosecutor agreed and moved the court accordingly, and only then was the kidnapper willing to confess to Susie's murder, as well as to the murders of the three other young people. He committed suicide hours later.

Today, Marietta says that working to stop the death penalty is the only way she can find to honor her daughter. As she explained to me and a group of students,

> "The loved ones who have been wrenched from our lives by violent crime deserve more

beautiful, noble, and honorable memorials than premeditated, barbaric, state-sanctioned killings, which create more victims and more grieving families, and which make us become that which we deplore—people who kill people—a horrendous insult to the memory of all our beloved victims."

Marietta did not always think and feel this way. She made a pilgrimage from grief and rage to hope for a less violent world.

◄o►

When you meet Robert "Renny" Cushing, he strikes you as a committed social activist and a politician in the pure sense of the word. He is a man who spends his days trying to think of the "common good," not simply his own interests. But Renny is more than a politician, even of the best, old-fashioned kind. He is a man who lost his father to murder and cleaned the walls of the place where it took place. And he is a man whose brother-in-law was also later murdered.

Now sixty years old, Renny is a child of the sixties who grew up in a liberal family, and all his life he has been a social activist. When I met him he had a full beard, and I remember seeing a picture of him and his father from the eighties, in which he wore a long, bushy moustache like Elliot Gould, or Dennis Hopper in *Easy Rider*.

Renny's father, Robert, was murdered a few days after the picture was taken. He was killed by two shotgun blasts fired by a stranger through the family's screen door. The two people who were convicted of the murder—an off-duty police officer and his wife—had animus against political liberals like the Cushings. They are now serving sentences of life without parole.

For his part, Renny has become a pioneer in the effort to bridge the death penalty abolition movement and the victims' rights movement. He served two terms in the New Hampshire House of Representatives, and he has testified before the US Congress and several state legislatures and addressed hundreds of audiences regarding victim opposition to the death penalty. While a lawmaker, he sponsored a measure that would have abolished the death penalty in his state. He now serves as Executive Director of Murder Victims' Families for Human Rights (MVFHR), and on their website he tells his story:

> Before my father's murder I had evolved a set of values that included a respect for life and an opposition to the death penalty. For me to change my beliefs because my father was murdered would only give more power to his killers, for they would then take not only his life but also his main legacy to me: the values he instilled. The same is true for society. If we let murderers turn us to murder, we give them

too much power. They succeed in bringing us to their way of thinking and acting, and we become what we say we abhor.

It is a good, clear argument and an honorable position to take. But it does not explain how a victim can stand for the abolition of the death penalty rather than seek retribution after the loss of a loved one. Meeting him, hearing his story, one wonders if Renny has a strange, prodigious gift for seeing issues at a distance. He wants no retribution, no eye for an eye. He wants to go ahead and "forgive the unforgivable." So it is useful to take a look at Renny's everyday life, as the journalist Claudia Dreyfus did, and see what it says about Renny Cushing's pilgrimage to Life Row.

> "After my father was killed, it seemed real important not to lose this house," Cushing explains. He is a slim man with a long melancholy face and a strong New England accent. "My dad and my grandfather built it. The killer may have taken my dad from us, but he wasn't going to take my roots, too. Staying here was one way of regaining control over my life. Besides, with time, the house has become something else. The floors that were once stained with my father's blood are also where my daughters learned how to walk."

. . .

"There's this myth out there that the families of victims need another killing for their healing," Cushing explains over coffee in his bright kitchen. A huge cat sleeps in a rocking chair, and his daughter Grace, 3, hums a Barney song in the next room. "The truth is, a lot of people are horrified by the very idea of an execution," he adds. "We know firsthand what violent death means, and we don't want to see society do it."

―◦―

Operating out of a small basement office in Cambridge, Massachusetts, with a staff of three, MVFHR's membership list includes Samuel R. Sheppard, son of Dr. Sam Sheppard, whose trial for the murder of his wife inspired two TV series and the movie *The Fugitive*.

As executive director of MVFHR, Renny travels the country and world speaking out against capital punishment. He publishes a newsletter and counsels victims' families, as well as the families of the condemned, about how to survive their trauma. He's good at his job. When the man who murdered former congressman Allard Lowenstein was unexpectedly freed by a New York judge in the year 2000, Cushing immediately visited Lowenstein's son, MVFHR member Thomas Lowenstein. "He just showed up and comforted me," says Lowenstein.

"He's lived through the difficulties of the criminal justice system himself and has a lot of insights on how you keep your values intact despite it." Lowenstein says both men count on humor to get through the bad times. "He's got just enough nuttiness not to take himself too seriously."

Cushing's achievements are substantial. He used the testimony of his members to defeat two bills that would have imposed capital punishment in Massachusetts. Across the country he has supported victims' families during trials, hearings, and executions—most recently in Nebraska, where MVFHR helped two murder survivors, both Quakers, who had opposed the death penalty for the killer of their relative and were refused a hearing because of their position. "There's this assumption that if you don't want more killing, you didn't really love the murdered person," says Cushing, who is a tireless advocate for better victim compensation laws. "We think that victims would be much better off with counseling and financial assistance, which they often need for funerals and legal help, than with an invitation to an execution." It was not a happy day for him when his bill to repeal the death penalty in New Hampshire stalled in the State Senate on April 17, 2014, after an incredible success in the House of Representatives. But happiness, he told me, had merely been postponed.

—<o>—

Julie Marie Welch was killed in the bombing of the Murrah Federal Building in Oklahoma City in 1995. She was twenty-three years old. In total, 168 people died in that bombing, and hundreds more were injured. There are countless victims if we consider the relatives and loved ones of the killed or injured.

Julie was what any parent desires: a brilliant young woman of great promise and solid values. She knew five languages and had majored in Spanish in college; she was working to help others as an interpreter for the Social Security Administration.

> Her father Bud's memory of that day is vivid; it cannot be otherwise:
>
> On the morning of April 19, 1995, my daughter, Julie Marie, went to St. Charles Borromeo for Mass at 7:00 AM. At 8:00 AM, she went to work at the Alfred P. Murrah Federal Building in Oklahoma City, where she assisted the Social Security Administration as a translator. At 9:00 AM, she went to the front of the building to greet a Mexican man who spoke no English. On their way back to her office in the rear of the building, a 5,000-pound fertilizer bomb was detonated, killing Julie and the client.
>
> In the months following Julie's death, I was one of many seeking vengeance for the people

who took my daughter. I turned to alcohol and cigarettes to ease my pain. I was angry with God for allowing this terrible thing to happen to me. But after several months, I began to hear Julie's voice. Years before, as a child herself, I remember her telling me that she thought that executions only taught children to hate.

My conviction is simple: More violence is not what Julie would have wanted. More violence will not bring Julie back. More violence only makes our society more violent.

This is how Bud sees things today. But it is not what he was thinking in the months after the killing. "I didn't even want a trial," he said. "I wanted the (expletives) fried."

Bud openly and widely shares that the killing of his daughter was killing him by keeping him enslaved to hatred. "After Julie was killed," he told me, "the rage, the revenge, the hate—you can't think of enough adjectives to describe what I felt like. When the President and the Attorney General announced that they would seek the death penalty for the perpetrators, that sounded wonderful to me, because here I had been crushed, I had been hurt, and that was the big fix. It took several months, but I came to realize that McVeigh's execution wouldn't help me. The death penalty is about revenge and hate, and those are the very reasons Julie and 167 others are dead today."

Bud had opposed the death penalty all his life, but when death touched his own life so brutally, he had been tempted to think differently.

"Three days after the bombing, as I watched Tim McVeigh being led out of the courthouse, I hoped someone in a high building with a rifle would shoot him dead . . . In fact, I'd have killed him myself if I'd had the chance." For a while, he felt that if he didn't seek the perpetrators' deaths, he somehow was guilty of not loving his daughter enough. In Rome, sitting at a table outside the Trattoria degli Amici, he told me:

"I went through that typical revenge that I was seeking for almost a year after the Oklahoma City bombing. And I was finally able to start thinking more rationally about things and became, once again, opposed to it."

If you talk to Bud now, he will explain, mincing no words, what purpose he believes the death penalty actually serves:

> The death penalty is a key part of prosecutors' being re-elected, because they, in their re-election campaigns, pound on the podium, and what they want to do actually is prove to us that they're the baddest ass in the jungle, if you will, and prove that they're tough on crime, by constantly talking about the death penalty.

How did this man come to think and feel this way—this

father whose daughter was murdered in an act so extreme and so senseless? "It was not an epiphany," he told me. "What I had—the most important thing that people have, after a loss—is time. One has to be given time to get rid of the initial anger. That's a very normal thing."

Bud now speaks about the death penalty to groups all over America, and he always tells the next part of the story at length:

> Unable to deal with the pain of Julie's death, I started self-medicating with alcohol until eventually the hangovers were lasting all day. Then, on a cold day in January 1996, I came to the bomb site, as I did every day, and I looked across the wasteland where the Murrah Building once stood. My head was splitting from drinking the night before and I thought, "I have to do something different, because what I'm doing isn't working."
>
> For the next few weeks I started to reconcile things in my mind, and finally concluded that it was revenge and hate that had killed Julie and the 167 others. Tim McVeigh and Terry Nichols had been against the US government for what happened in Waco, Texas in 1993, and seeing what they'd done with their vengeance, I knew I had to send mine in a different direction. Shortly

afterward I started speaking out against the death penalty.

I also remembered that shortly after the bombing I'd seen a news report on Tim McVeigh's father, Bill. He was shown stooping over a flowerbed, and when he stood up I could see that he'd been physically bent over in pain. I recognized it because I was feeling that pain, too.

Bud told me, "Yes, it was not an epiphany, but it was an epiphany, too. I realized what the McVeigh family went through. Can you imagine? To be the family of the one responsible for the killing of 168 people?"

Ironically, it was the kindness of Bill McVeigh that helped Bud to break through and to make his own decision to live on life row. Here is Bud's account of visiting the McVeigh family home, where he spent time with both Bill and Tim's younger sister, Jennifer.

Earlier, when we were in the garden, Bill had asked me, "Bud, are you able to cry?" I'd told him, "I don't usually have a problem crying." His reply was, "I can't cry, even though I've got a lot to cry about." But later, sitting at the kitchen table, looking at Tim's photo, a big tear rolled down his face. It was the love of a father for a son.

When I got ready to leave I shook Bill's hand, then extended it to Jennifer, but she just grabbed me and threw her arms around me. She was the same sort of age as Julie but felt so much taller. I don't know which one of us started crying first. Then I held her face in my hands and said, "Look, honey, the three of us are in this for the rest of our lives. I don't want your brother to die, and I'll do everything I can to prevent it." As I walked away from the house I realized that until that moment I had walked alone, but now a tremendous weight had lifted from my shoulders. I had found someone who was a bigger victim of the Oklahoma bombing than I was, because while I can speak in front of thousands of people and say wonderful things about Julie, if Bill McVeigh meets a stranger he probably doesn't even say he had a son.

About a year before the execution I found it in my heart to forgive Tim McVeigh. It was a release for me rather than for him.

Relatives of the Oklahoma City bombing victims were granted the right to watch Timothy McVeigh's execution. Since the case involved so many victims, the federal government made arrangements for the execution to be shown in a much bigger place than the typical small room near the death chamber, via closed-circuit television. But an overwhelming majority of the families—in fact 88 percent, including Bud Welch—chose not to participate, not to watch. In this way, the argument that an execution serves as a brutal but necessary act of closure for the victims' families was firmly and convincingly rejected.

—◦—

The family members of murder victims are not just survivors, but victims too. They face a life's journey—a never-ending pilgrimage—of healing. But Art, Marietta, Renny, and Bud prove that it can be done. None of them could be faulted for feeling rage and hatred, or for desiring the deaths of those responsible for their pain. But instead they have courageously chosen to move past these feelings. In their fight against the death penalty, each of them has found a path through suffering, and a way to honor the loved ones they lost: by making the world a better, less violent place.

10.
Between Life and Death: Buddhism, Hinduism, Judaism, Islam, and Christianity

Since the various world religions exist in so many forms—across different schools, organizations, and areas—it is impossible to say that any of them has a unified message on the ultimate punishment. On the one hand, many of their core teachings would seem to argue strongly against taking a life for a life, but on the other, there are plenty of counterexamples from history of religious institutions supporting the death penalty with bone-shaking vigor.

◄○►

The Dalai Lama had just finished speaking at an event on the Capitoline Hill in Rome when I sought him out and asked him to be one of the first signatories of the Community of Sant'Egidio's Appeal for a Moratorium on the Death Penalty. He accepted immediately and signed in earth-green ink, which came as no surprise. Who more than the Dalai Lama is identified around the world with the need to respect life?

Indeed, all schools of Buddhism emphasize respect for life in all its forms. Though the Buddha did not specifically address capital punishment in his teachings, he encouraged his adherents not to do anything that could harm others, saying, "An action, even if it brings benefit to oneself, cannot be considered a good action if it causes physical and mental pain to another being."

The respect for life that permeates Buddhism is inextricably connected to the principle of *samsara*, the infinitely repeating cycle of birth, suffering, death, and rebirth. Buddhists believe that samsara is the world's nervous system, and when the death penalty is applied, both the soul of the person whose life is taken and the soul of the person who takes that life are negatively affected. It follows that trying to gain recompense for evil and even for violent death by inflicting more death simply causes a greater imbalance; only rehabilitation can restore balance and harmony in this world and the world of the spirit.

But, of course, the devil is in the details: in many countries where Buddhism is influential, such as Thailand and Japan, the death penalty is still thriving in spirit and in practice.

What accounts for this contradiction? One explanation may be that there is a wide disparity between the practices of Buddhist monastic orders and lay Buddhist followers (as in any religion). In their article "Mercy and Punishment: Buddhism and the Death Penalty," criminology professors Leanne Fiftal Alarid and Hsiao-Ming

Wang argue that while "the death penalty is inconsistent with Buddhist teachings," historical reality is more complicated:

> Buddhist doctrines hold nonviolence and compassion for all life in high regard. The First Precept of Buddhism requires individuals to abstain from injuring or killing all living creatures and Buddha's teaching restricts Buddhist monks from any political involvement. Using historical documents and interviews with contemporary authorities on Buddhist doctrine, our research uncovered a long history of political involvement by Buddhist monks and Buddhist support of violence.

The website ProCon.org gathers opinions from different cultures and religions on capital punishment. In the case of Buddhism, one voice on the "pro" side is that of Tomoko Sasaki, a former member of the Japanese Diet. Writing in a *Washington Post* article titled "Why Japan Still Has the Death Penalty," he evokes "retribution" to justify his opinion: "A basic teaching [in Japanese Buddhism] is retribution. If someone evil does something bad, he has to atone with his own life."

Sasaki assumes that capital punishment restores balance in karmic terms. But in reality, the death penalty creates a double negative: one life is lost, and then another follows. Capital punishment, seen in this way, is a violent disruption to the possibility of balancing different karmas and improving the world by favoring mercy and life. The flow and intercommunication of the reproductive karma, the supportive karma, the obstructive karma, and the destructive karma are dealt great blows by every death sentence.

When the Dalai Lama subscribed to the appeal I submitted on behalf of the Community of Sant'Egidio, he also submitted this message, read at an event organized by the Peace Center on April 9, 1999:

> The death penalty fulfills a preventive function, but it is also very clearly a form of revenge. It is an especially severe form of punishment because it is so final. The human life is ended and the executed person is deprived of the opportunity to change, to restore the harm done or compensate for it. Before advocating execution we should consider whether criminals are intrinsically negative and harmful people . . . The answer, I believe, is definitely not. However horrible the act they have committed, I believe that everyone has the potential to improve and correct themselves. Therefore, I am optimistic that it remains possible to deter criminal activity, and

prevent such harmful consequences of such acts in society, without having to resort to the death penalty.

—◦—

"An eye for an eye makes the whole world blind"—this adage, generally attributed to Gandhi, is the remark quoted most often by opponents of the death penalty. And yet in Hinduism we are on the same contradictory ground as in Buddhism. On the one hand, India resumed executions in November 2012 after almost a decade of a *de facto* moratorium; on the other hand, there have been only two executions there over the past two years. When you compare that number to India's giant population of 1.3 billion people, the death penalty starts to seem practically nonexistent.

Those who do support the death penalty give reasons that are distinctly different from the ones we generally hear in the West. The founder of the Hare Krishna movement, Srila Prabhupada, explained in *Bhagavad-Gita As It Is* (1968) that a murderer should be condemned to death so that "in his next life he will not have to suffer for the great sin he has committed."

Samvidananda Saraswati, the head of Kailash Ashram, offers the counter perspective:

> There is a general feeling that Hinduism is full of compassion and forgiveness . . . Therefore,

> taking the life of a human being is a very big
> issue for us . . . Our scriptures and Vedas do
> not favor capital punishment. They advocate
> the principle of nonviolence.

Another word for this "principle of nonviolence"
in Hinduism is "Ahimsa," which literally means "non-
harm." Gandhi, who was one of the most famous
advocates of Ahimsa, explained, "In its negative form,
[Ahimsa] means not injuring any living being, whether
by body or mind. I may not therefore hurt the person of
any wrong-doer, or bear any ill will to him and so cause
mental suffering."

This attitude is very nearly inscribed in the Indian
Constitution, which says that the death penalty is to be
applied only "in the rarest of rare cases." And if it were
up to some of India's founding fathers—including the
Constitution's main architect, Babasaheb Ambedkar—
there would be no death penalty at all. Ambedkar
acknowledged that while people may not always practice
nonviolence, "[t]hey certainly adhere to the principle of
nonviolence as a moral mandate which they ought to
observe as far as they possibly can." For this reason he
concluded that "the proper thing for this country to do is
to abolish the death sentence altogether."

—◦—

Like Hinduism and Buddhism, Judaism exhibits many contradictions when it comes to the death penalty. In the Hebrew Bible and the Talmud, the death penalty is both legitimate and widespread: thirty-six crimes in the Hebrew Bible are punishable by death, including idol worship, profanation of the Sabbath, adultery, incest, and public incitement to apostasy. And the Mishnah lists the methods of execution (Sanhedrin 7:1) as slaying by the sword, stoning, burning, and strangling.

But Jewish texts also place limits on the way a death sentence can be administered. First, there must be a trial before a Sanhedrin, an ancient Jewish liturgical and criminal court, whose jury comprised twenty-three judges in capital cases. Furthermore, at least two witnesses are required to testify both that they witnessed the crime for which the defendant is on trial and that they had warned him or her in advance that the crime was punishable by execution. Not even the defendant's own confession is to be accepted as evidence.

And while Orthodox Judaism holds that in theory the death penalty is the correct and just punishment for some crimes, the Mishnah stresses that it is not to be administered lightly. A famous passage says,

> A Sanhedrin that puts a man to death once in seven years is called destructive. Rabbi Eliezer ben Azariah says: even once in seventy years. Rabbi Akiba and Rabbi Tarfon say: had we

> been in the Sanhedrin none would ever have
> been put to death. Rabbi Simeon ben Gamaliel
> says: they would have multiplied shedders of
> blood in Israel. (Mattot 1:10)

Undoubtedly this reluctance to administer the death
penalty stems from the belief in Judaism that human life
is sacred. In his book *Judaism and Human Rights*, Rabbi
David Rosen elaborates:

> The Mishnah powerfully articulates...the
> human right to life and progeny. Precisely that
> sacred right to life resultant from being created
> in the image of God, is that which serves to
> make the concomitant demands on us to
> respect and protect the life of the other.

Perhaps because the taking of a life is such a serious
thing in Judaism, some argue that humans can only
administer the death penalty if and when their justice
system is perfect. In a 1932 article, Rabbi Isaac Herzog,
who went on to become the first chief rabbi of the State
of Israel, wrote that the Sanhedrin—and, by extension,
capital punishment—could only be restored in the
Messianic age, when divine law and human law would
become one; until then, he said, the death penalty should
not be administered.

Indeed, when the State of Israel was founded, its

legislature chose to rule not as a Sanhedrin but as a secular body. Furthermore, the legislature abolished the death penalty in 1954, except as a punishment for genocide or treason committed in wartime. Strictly speaking, in the history of modern Israel, capital punishment has been administered only once during peacetime, to the Nazi bureaucrat Adolf Eichmann in 1962.

In the United States, both the Central Conference of American Rabbis (CCAR) and the Union for Reform Judaism (URJ) publicly oppose the death penalty. The CCAR formally rejected the death penalty "[b]oth in concept and in practice" in 1979. And the URJ has stated, "We believe that there is no crime for which the taking of human life by society is justified, and that it is the obligation of society to evolve other methods in dealing with crime."

◄◦►

Mainstream Islam generally favors forgiveness. In *Policing Muslim Communities*, Farrukh B. Hakeem, M.R. Haberfeld, and Arvind Verma write, "Contrary to the common perception that is widely prevalent, Islamic laws are essentially preventive and not based solely on harsh punishment as a first resort; rather, the harsh punishments are implemented as a last resort."

Specifically, Islamic law applies the death penalty to two groups of crime. The first is intentional murder.

In these cases the families of the victims are allowed to choose between capital punishment for the offender and monetary compensation—or they may simply forgive. And their decision is binding on the state.

The second group of crimes that may incur the death penalty, according to the Qur'an, is *fasad fil-ardh*, which is defined as spreading mischief in the community or the land. *Fasad fil-ardh* can have a broad meaning or a strict one. In authoritarian regimes, it can be a way for rulers to control opposition, spread terror, or eliminate political opponents by bringing exaggerated or invented charges against opponents or enemies. Treason, apostasy, terrorism, rape, piracy, adultery, and homosexual activity all may fall under *fasad fil-ardh*.

The BBC reported on the declaration of Imad-ad-Dean Ahmad, the President of the Minaret of Freedom Institute, who two months after September 11 had this to say about the death penalty:

> The views of American Muslims on the death penalty vary somewhat, but the range is narrow compared to the enormous disagreements among Christians. All Muslims accept the permissibility of the death penalty because it is addressed in the Qur'an. However, our views range from those who would apply it for a moderately short list of crimes (short compared to the enormous list of capital crimes in the

Old Testament), to those who would apply it to a somewhat shorter list still, and finally, to those who would call for a moratorium on the death penalty in America altogether.

Although the Qur'an sanctions capital punishment in some cases, many Muslim countries have abolished the death penalty, including Albania, Turkey, and Uzbekistan. Other countries are abolitionist in practice if not in law: Algeria, Tajikistan, and Tunisia, to name a few. And still others are taking official steps toward a legal moratorium: for example, in February 2013, a strong parliamentary initiative began in Morocco and almost 180 MPs organized a Moroccan Parliamentarian Network Against the Death Penalty with the goal of outlawing capital punishment.

My friend Siti Musdah Mulia, researcher and professor at the Indonesian Institute of Sciences and a lecturer on Islamic Political Thought at Syarif Hidayatullah State Islamic University in Jakarta, is fighting for an end of the death penalty in Indonesia, the most populous Muslim country in the world. When we were together in Aosta Valley, where the Italian government named her "Woman of the Year" in 2009, she explained to me that, in her view, "Islamic teaching is not compatible with the death penalty."

She draws her argument from Imam al-Ghazali, a Muslim theologian, jurist, and philosopher who died in 1111 AD, and who identified "five necessities," or *al-darûriyyât al-khamsa*, that Muslim law must protect: religion, life, intellect, offspring, and property. In the *al-darûriyyât al-khamsa*, Mulia finds a basis for something like a declaration of human rights: the right to religious freedom, the right to life, the right to express opinions freely, the right to reproductive health, and the right to property. Because capital punishment contravenes the right to life, she argues that it is antithetical to Islam and should be abolished.

—◇—

The relationship between Christianity and the death penalty is similarly inconsistent. In the Old Testament, of course, there is an abundance of references to crimes punishable by death. The Book of Leviticus contains a long list that is still quoted, and not just by fundamentalist Christians; among other sins, idolatry, adultery, incest, homosexual activity, and bestiality are punishable by death. But there are different lines of teaching between which we must negotiate. For example, God marks Cain to warn others against killing him, even though he has murdered his brother. God also forbids David to build His house on Earth because he "shed blood abundantly, and . . . made great wars." (1 Chronicles 22:8)

While the New Testament does not explicitly condemn the death penalty, its attitude toward violence is more straightforwardly negative than the Old Testament's. Jesus preached a message of love and compassion, famously saying, "Thou shalt love thy neighbor as thyself." And in his Sermon on the Mount he stipulated that this love should extend even to our enemies (Matthew 5:43–47). He also opposed revenge: "Ye have heard that it hath been said, An eye for an eye, and a tooth for a tooth: But I say unto you, that ye resist not evil: but whosoever shall smite thee on thy right cheek, turn to him the other also." (Matthew 5:38–39)

A strong opposition to violence marked the first three centuries of Christian life. Church Fathers such as Athenagoras of Athens, Hippolytus of Rome, Tertullian, and Origen opposed Christian involvement with executions and the death penalty, arguing that violence went against Jesus's teachings. For the same reason many early Christians refused to serve in the Roman army, which sometimes resulted in their executions.

But that all changed with the Edict of Milan in 313–14 AD, which legalized Christianity in the Roman Empire, dramatically altering Christianity's relationship to the state and, by extension, to state-sponsored violence. In 314 AD, the Council of Arles, a representative meeting of Christian bishops, convened to discuss military service, among other things. They came to the consensus that, "[c]oncerning those who lay down their weapons in peacetime, be it resolved that they be excluded from fellowship." While this canon has been interpreted in various ways, the most obvious interpretation would seem to be that the punishment for military desertion during peacetime is excommunication from the Church—a far cry from the early days of Christianity.

The legitimacy of violence soon made its way into Christian theology. Under his Just War theory, theologian and bishop Augustine of Hippo held that war was morally justified if it met certain conditions. Centuries later, Thomas Aquinas argued in favor of the death penalty, writing in *Summa contra Gentiles*:

> The fact that the evil ones, as long as they live, can be corrected from their errors does not prohibit that they may be justly executed, for the danger which threatens from their way of life is greater and more certain than the good which may be expected from their improvement.

Christian support for the death penalty continued for many centuries as part of a broader Western trend, with both Protestant and Catholic supporters. But with the Second Vatican Council in the 1960s, the Catholic Church moved closer to the early spirit of Christianity. In 1969, Pope Paul VI abolished the death penalty in the Vatican State, and in 1975 he appealed to Spain's dictator, Francisco Franco, asking him to commute the death sentences of five convicted Spanish terrorists (who were later executed by firing squad).

Although the Catechism of the Catholic Church still "does not exclude recourse to the death penalty, if this is the only possible way of effectively defending human lives against the unjust aggressor," recent popes have reinforced Paul VI's opposition to capital punishment. In 1999, John Paul II called for an international consensus to abolish the "cruel and unnecessary" death penalty, saying, "Modern society has the means of protecting itself, without definitively denying criminals the chance to reform." Pope Benedict XVI, receiving the participants in the International Meeting of Ministers of Justice promoted by the Community of Sant'Egidio on November 30, 2011, spoke of encouraging "the political and legislative initiatives being promoted in a growing number of countries to eliminate the death penalty."

Most recently, Pope Francis has spoken out against the death penalty in a message to the International Association of Penal Law in October 2014, where he called upon "[a]ll Christians and people of goodwill . . . to struggle . . . for abolition of the death penalty, whether legal or illegal, and in all its forms...out of respect for the human dignity of persons deprived of their liberty." He went on to say, "It is impossible to imagine that states today cannot make use of another means than capital punishment to defend peoples' lives from an unjust aggressor." He could not have been any clearer.

Another Christian denomination that has maintained a constant front against the death penalty is the Church of England. I remember a conversation I had with the Primate of the Church of England, Rowan Williams, in 2007. It was a few weeks before the UN General Assembly reaffirmed the resolution on a death penalty moratorium. When we reached the issue of capital punishment, he called for change:

The death penalty is one of those things which always speaks against hope . . .

> In so many countries where the death penalty exists, it is not the death penalty alone, it is the whole environment that grows up around it: the environment of the condemned cell, of the long periods where many people wait for execution. I have been in countries where people waited twenty years and have been on death row for twenty years. It is inhumane. I've also been in countries where it's quite clear that certain races, certain classes, certain sections of the population are much more likely to receive the death penalty than others. So we need to remember—it's not only the infliction of death itself, it is everything that goes with it that dehumanizes.

I asked him if he wanted to launch an appeal to different audiences around the world to abolish the death penalty, and he said, "The challenge I would want to put is this:

can we truly affirm human dignity for everyone? Even if it's difficult, even if it is in some ways risky, so that we can honestly say, we can say with integrity: this is a culture that takes life seriously."

—◦—

It is the work of all the world's religions to look seriously at life in all its vivid complexity. And so must we take the arguments and questions raised by these religions seriously, without resort to simplistic views of their arcs through history. Although none of the world's religions can be said to irrefutably oppose the death penalty, they all contain teachings that celebrate life and human dignity above all else. And though it may be a long time yet before all the world's religions unequivocally denounce the death penalty, more and more followers are speaking out against it and effecting change. Their work keeps the flicker of hope alive, even in the darkest times, for those who are living in any place and according to any custom.

11.
The UN Resolution: Getting to "No"

Just as it is strange that the modern efforts to do away with the death penalty are associated with a child ruler—Pietro Leopoldo of Tuscany—it's strange too that efforts to do away with the death penalty in our own time will forever be linked to a cruel dictator: Saddam Hussein.

Saddam, of course, was sentenced to death by the provisional government in Iraq after his capture in the second Iraq War. At the time, the death sentence was a foregone conclusion, even a banality, by the standards of a period marked by the US military's "shock and awe" strategy. And yet the actual execution of Saddam, on December 30, 2006, provoked indignation around the world. The photograph of the ousted dictator hanging by a noose spread across the web on computers and mobile phones; a crude video of the execution could be found online, too, made on a cell phone by one the executioners, whose laughter can be heard in the background. Never before had so many people seen what an execution looks like—and how barbaric it can be.

The images, together with the execution itself, sparked

revulsion in several forms. Here execution could be seen as a brutal act, as cruelty carried out in the third millennium, as in Mississippi a century earlier, or in Nuremburg after World War II. It was seen as a crude and ultimately ineffective revenge inflicted by the victors. Even those who considered Saddam an evil man and a war criminal might hesitate and be sickened by what they saw. And in the Arab world, especially, so brutal an execution—carried out during a sacred time in the Islamic calendar—was seen as an act of revenge and aggression on the part of the Western-sponsored interim government, not as an act of international justice.

For the movement against the death penalty, Saddam's execution was an unwanted opportunity, as the atrocities and spectacular executions in Iraq and Syria today may prove to be also. A moratorium on executions in wartime Iraq had been called for, so as to foster reconciliation, rather than retaliation, among the Iraqi people. Nevertheless, it was an opportunity—and a profound turning point. With a meaningful part of public opinion now running against the death penalty, those of us working for a moratorium rallied our efforts, and this time those working for full abolition, who generally opposed moratoria as halfway measures, did not stand in the way. All uncertainties and divisions within the movement subsided, everyone came together, and a predominantly European movement became a worldwide movement with the clear goal of a UN resolution against the death penalty backed by a broad, global coalition of member states. Writing this, I am reminded of a process that lasted months, culminating in a massive change.

Since the 1990s there had been a deep division between NGOs and states that favored the abolition of the death penalty and those that favored a moratorium. Africa was largely retentionist. So was the United States, whose lawmakers considered the country in a class by itself, even though a good number of individual US states were set against capital punishment. Countries in Asia applied the death penalty with vigor, while Europe became the first continent whose countries (except for Belarus) banned the death penalty without exception.

In 1998, the European Union prepared its second resolution calling for a moratorium on the death penalty and took it to the UN General Assembly, even though there remained internal divisions among European member states. After the EU's presentation, Singapore led a rebuttal. Egypt and others, on behalf of Asian, Arab, Muslim, and Caribbean countries, pushed through "killer amendments" that contradicted the spirit of the draft Resolution, and threatened even more. They rejected the EU resolution on the grounds that it would interfere in their internal judicial affairs, and tried to label it as the expression of a neocolonialist notion of human rights. Italy proposed a preamble quoting both Articles Two and Three of the UN Charter so that a compromise could be found, but the EU stuck firm to its original text and no mediation proved possible. So the resolution was withdrawn without coming up for a vote.

From that moment on, the Community of Sant'Egidio worked to mend the split between the abolitionist and pro-moratorium factions. And we sought to correct the impression that the call for a change of policy on the death penalty was an act of European arrogance, or an attempt to impose a neocolonialist vision of human rights on less powerful countries.

The Appeal for a Universal Moratorium, which had garnered several million signatures and support from leaders of all political leanings, had created a sort of worldwide moral front against capital punishment.

In 2001, the First World Congress Against the Death Penalty took place in Strasbourg. This was an initiative of the French ECPM, supported by the French government. It led to a meeting of anti-death penalty activists from different parts of the world. Even if the conference was less global than European and francophone, it was an important step. It led to a meeting, in May 2002, of the leaders of some of the main NGOs and movements opposing the death penalty. We met at Sant'Egidio's headquarters in Rome.

As in Julius Caesar's time, Rome was a sort of cradle of the world. In a seventeenth-century building in Trastevere that housed a quiet garden, The World Coalition Against the Death Penalty was born from thirteen different movements, including ECPM, Sant'Egidio, Amnesty

International, FIDH, PRI, NACDP, HoC, and DP Focus, among others.

There were few pictures taken in the tiny garden of Sant'Egidio's headquarters. There was no official photographer. Nevertheless, that day turned out to be one of history's small turning points. The World Coalition devised a strategy to coordinate grassroots efforts and lend support to smaller organizations. It instituted an annual World Day Against the Death Penalty on November 30. With Cities for Life - Cities Against the Death Penalty, we sought to demonstrate the vigor of opinion against the death penalty in officially retentionist states through events in prominent cities, and so to create internal tension in societies that continue to implement the death penalty, so that a call for change would come from within civil society. The peaceful war machine of November 30 had been already tested, so we established the first World Day on that year.

Now some of us had a clear agenda: to obtain a successful UN resolution. And all of us had a common goal, the abolition of capital punishment. Despite the differences between our two paths, we could now count on more effective tools and empower each other.

How was it possible to create a new process that would lead to the final approval of a UN Resolution in the UN General Assembly's Third Committee, dedicated to social, humanitarian, and cultural development, where a Resolution had been withdrawn before the vote in 1998?

The process involved politics, some strategizing, some compromise, some good timing, and some good luck. But it was rooted in our confidence in the cause, our sense that the death penalty is wrong and that more and more the people of the world are recognizing this and speaking up about it. The gray areas of the death penalty were slowly turning to white.

As far as the UN was concerned—and as I had anticipated—Amnesty International, the pioneer group campaigning against the death penalty, had favored proceeding slowly and cautiously, waiting until there was a clear majority of one hundred countries ratifying the Second Optional Protocol to the International Covenant on Civil and Political Rights, still the only binding international treaty on the issue, before taking it to the General Assembly. At a rate of maybe five new ratifications per year, this would have taken ten years or more; the actual rate was—and remains—far slower.

The World Coalition had favored the same approach until 2007. Meanwhile, Hands Off Cain, an offshoot of the Radical Party in Italy and the force behind the first (withdrawn) UN resolution, used its political clout to urge Italian government leaders to take the issue back to the UN "at any cost." The Prodi government and its foreign minister, Massimo D'Alema, caved to the pressure and started engaging the institution, but not everyone agreed with the notion of hastily presenting a solely Italian resolution in the sixty-first session of the General Assembly, which was drawing to a close around Easter. Somehow, also in direct, confidential contacts with the Community of Sant'Egidio, Italy's Ministry of Foreign Affairs showed interest in focusing efforts on the next session of the General Assembly, the sixty-second, which was to be opened in September of that year.

The Community of Sant'Egidio was in favor of returning to the UN, but only with a well-prepared international and institutional campaign. So we'd need to organize one.

Hands Off Cain pushed its position during the Third World Congress against the Death Penalty in Paris in February 2007. The leader of the Radical Party, Marco Pannella, attended, even though Hands Off Cain, after co-founding the Coalition, went years without playing an active role in it. The signal given by the presence of the Italian radical leader was clear. Amnesty International, fearing a second (third) defeat at the UN, remained skeptical. The Congress's final document, which defined the Moratorium as part of a worldwide strategy for abolishing capital punishment, met with serious resistance. Eric Prokosh, long of Amnesty International and now with the World Congress, prepared an abstract of the text, which he submitted to me in advance and which I helped to edit, calling for a commitment on the part of the international movement to the pursuit of a universal moratorium, but it was not approved. Rather, it was in danger of being crossed off, and the conflict threatened to break ties between international initiatives and the actions of anti-death penalty movements on the civil and institutional levels in the year in which it was likely that the battle would finally reach the UN in earnest. Its absence would have marked a repudiation of the initiative that was about to travel from Italy and the EU to the UN General Assembly in New York.

Speedy Rice of Death Penalty Focus and I tried to mediate the dispute through triangular conference calls between Rome, London, and New York, along with the London representatives of Amnesty International, Florence Bellivier of Penal Reform International (PRI), Eleonore Morel of the *Federation International de Droites de l'Homme* (FIDH), and Hands Off Cain. Finally, we settled on wording that enabled the World Coalition to support every effort to ask for a special effort from the member states at drafting a "successful" resolution and to do it "as soon as possible." One last call to Amnesty International in New York and the deal was clinched.

A UN resolution must be sponsored by one or more member states. Because the 1998 resolution had been sponsored by the EU—and had met with criticisms of neocolonialism—we were looking for a different approach.

Hands Off Cain continued to work hard, especially pressuring the Italian government, which appeared to have ruled out seeking a Resolution at the UN before May. In March, a Declaration of Intent drafted by Italy was approved unanimously in Brussels by the twenty-seven countries of the EU and seemed to be leading to an international initiative against the death penalty. Inside the Italian Parliament, members of the Radical Party obtained a motion approved unanimously by the Commission for Foreign Affairs of the Chamber.

Italy, in short, was working to attain European consensus. It garnered support right away from France (led by Nicolas Sarkozy) and Germany (led by Angela Merkel), and sponsored the Declaration of Intent, which received widespread approval. It now had to develop consensus in the European Parliament. It stepped into the background and left the initiative to Germany and then to Portugal, which assumed the EU presidency beginning in July. Hands Off Cain also knew that chances for success with a Resolution were much better in the second semester than the first. But they took the approach that pressure today could help bring about success tomorrow. In Italian, there's a saying: "Questa e' la politica, bellezza!" "That's politics, my dear!"

At the World Coalition's General Assembly in Brussels that June, the picture was still unclear. Initially the key issues of the fall and year-end campaigns centered on targeting Asia's retentionist countries. On the agenda was the approval of materials and tool-kits to be sent to the entire movement as a start to the mobilization that was to peak on the World Day Against the Death Penalty (after the first year it was decided that there would be two "world" events: one on October 10, the World Day Against the Death Penalty—later recognized by the EU as European Day Against the Death Penalty—and the other on November 30, Cities for Life Day). Asia was the center of the campaign, the graphics, and all the leaflets.

It was clear to me that it would have been a mistake to disconnect the grassroots movement from the member states' strength of action under such circumstances. Sant'Egidio and Amnesty International took a different approach, affirming (after lunch) that the Resolution at the UN had become a key step for the eventual abolition of the death penalty. In the space of one day—one afternoon—members of the two groups agreed upon a radical change of strategy, making the Resolution a first priority and assigning the World Coalition a proactive role in the international lobbying effort. From then on, we held a weekly conference call to coordinate our efforts and implement a new method of operating. Amnesty International was bearing the expenses for the conference calls and keeping track of the different efforts made. Each organization was free to direct its activities towards the countries where they would be most effective.

In August we held a crucial meeting in Lisbon to draft the plan. On a splendid summer day at the Foreign Ministry, Portugal's top human rights official sat at one end of a table around the rest of which sat representatives

of Amnesty International for the World Coalition, Hands
Off Cain, and myself for Sant'Egidio. We reached agreement on several points. The main one was this: The work
for a Resolution was not to be merely a European initiative
but a truly international one. At least ten co-sponsoring
countries had to be drawn from five continents. The EU
would help but would not officially take the lead. If possible, Russia and South Africa were to be involved from the
beginning, together with countries like Mexico, Brazil,
Angola, and Gabon (which had just agreed to abolish the
death penalty); Rwanda, Burundi and Cambodia (which
had experienced genocide); and the Philippines, East
Timor, and New Zealand. In this way, the Resolution
would have credible promoters and influential regional
backers from its beginning. Canada had just pulled out as
a co-sponsor, announcing its support but backing down
from playing a proactive role.

Things were moving ahead—but we were still anxious
about the difficulty of obtaining majority support for a
Resolution in the UN General Assembly. In September we
reviewed the draft resolution once again. And again. And
again, as it underwent revision by sponsoring countries.

Somehow it was a special opportunity to join all the
efforts and lobbying possibilities that we had.

On June 18, 2007, the Second International Conference
of Ministers of Justice, organized by the Community of
Sant'Egidio, had taken place at Julius Caesar Hall on
the Capitoline Hill. On one wall there is a plaque that

marks the decision taken in 1849 by the new Repubblica Romana—a Rome temporarily free of papal rule, before the national consolidation of Italy—to set aside the death penalty. So we were in good company. A large number of officials and MPs from abolitionist and "retention-ist" countries in Africa were in attendance.[70] The large African turnout had a sort of ripple effect; together with Sant'Egidio's humanitarian activities in Africa, it increased a process of visits and institutional talks between African nations and in Rome that continues to this day.

Our annual interfaith World Meeting of Dialogue and Prayer for Peace in Naples in October 2007 offered another occasion for countries like Kazakhstan to enter the process of ending the death penalty, preparing the way for one more vote in favor of a UN Resolution in the process. As a large country in central Asia, Kazakhstan created momentum for other countries of Central Asia like Kyrgyzstan and Tajikistan, to vote in support of the Resolution. Uzbekistan was there already, thanks to the work of the brave Mothers Against the Death Penalty and their allies.

The text of the Resolution was reviewed by the original promoters of the initiative. It gained momentum and new co-sponsors after we limited references to the abolition of the death penalty as our final objective to a single, deci-sive sentence, avoiding a tone that might be considered "too aggressive." The argument that the Resolution was "European and neocolonialist" was countered by the large number of sponsors: eighty-nine countries, the highest number ever.

Now was the time to act. Whoever had contacts, prestige, and cards to play, should lay them down.

In late October 2007, some of us traveled to UN headquarters. Don't imagine crowds—we were a small group working with a meager budget. For several years we had focused our efforts on the approval of a Resolution against the death penalty in the General Assembly. Now the opportunity was at hand.

We brought with us five million signatures gathered by Sant'Egidio in 153 countries, and another 200,000 gathered by the World Coalition—all calling for a moratorium on capital punishment and the eventual abolition of the death penalty altogether.

The number of co-sponsors was growing, but it was hard to know what the real situation was. The prominent Italian minister Emma Bonino, one of the founders of Hands Off Cain, made remarks to the Italian press suggesting that the Resolution was at risk. She was worried that the European front would be divided at the time of presentation, or that the Resolution might be withdrawn before the vote as in 1998, or might not be presented at all. Or something else.

These were frantic hours for all of us. Myself, I was walking, calling, meeting, drinking coffee, checking in with each UN member state, synching up with the other members of our delegation, organizing the meeting with the President of the General Assembly, talking to the media, and learning to use a BlackBerry for the first time, out of necessity. Jetlagged, I couldn't sleep anyway, so I spent the nights trying to get in touch with allies in Italy and other countries. It was worth it. More than anything, I was awaiting word about the fate of our Resolution. Each of us in the delegation worked for two days without stopping. I'll never forget Speedy Rice, a distinguished professor and lawyer, overloaded with files and papers, as humble as his goal was lofty.

I had finally succeeded in arranging a meeting with the president of the UN General Assembly, Srgjan Kerim of Macedonia, for November 1. He had already met Emma Bonino. So it was clear to him that this was a meeting of peculiar importance. That day we delivered the five million signatures in a giant, hand-tooled leather book featuring signatures from 153 countries and signatures of many prominent people calling for an end to the death penalty.

Our delegation included Sister Helen Prejean; Speedy Rice, representing on this occasion the National Association for the Advancement of Colored People; Renny Cushing of Murder Victims' Families Against the Death Penalty; Yvonne Terlingen, Amnesty International's representative to the UN; Elizabeth Zitrin of Death Penalty Focus; and the family members of crime victims. I led the delegation on behalf of the Community of Sant'Egidio. With the signatures, we hoped to make clear that our work was not just European or neocolonialist; our goals enjoyed broad support from ordinary people in countries all over the world.

The next day, November 2, 2007, Resolution 62/149, "A Moratorium on the Use of the Death Penalty," was presented to the Third Committee of the UN General Assembly, where it would be put up for a vote in the middle of the month.

Ten states sponsored the Resolution, including Brazil, Portugal, New Zealand, Gabon, East Timor, and even Russia, which had employed the death penalty both under the czars and during the Communist era. All told, the total number of co-sponsors was eighty-seven (to become eighty-nine before the final vote)—the largest number of co-sponsors in the history of the General Assembly, I was told.

I returned to Rome hopeful and relieved that the first step had been taken. I followed the development of the issue through contacts in the missions to the UN of Italy and other countries. At Sant'Egidio, there are people who have good contacts with leaders in various parts of the world, the outcome of long lasting efforts at peacemaking and humanitarian work. So many of those friends worked hard to bring their national leaders around, or, in some cases—Liberia, Malawi, Niger, the Democratic Republic of Congo, and Eritrea, for example—to persuade them to abstain rather than voting against. We worked with counterparts in South Africa, Mozambique, Kyrgyzstan,

Guatemala, and other countries to encourage a yes vote. And we double-checked with friends in Albania, Burundi, and Rwanda, making sure their support remained. Actions and intentions all over the world were building to the climax we had worked so hard to achieve.

As an example of the felicitous timing that bolstered our efforts, and of the peculiar "diplomacy" the Community of Sant'Egidio engaged in, it is useful to mention that Gabon was one of the countries that worked hardest at putting the results of the Second "Africa for Life" Conference in Rome into practice.

The pledges made on that occasion by Justice Minister Martin Mabala were translated into legislative actions, and abolition came sooner than expected, thanks to the intervention of President Omar Bongo Ondimba, who officially thanked Sant'Egidio for its commitment and efforts to promote the abolition of the death penalty. But the diplomatic effort, conducted through direct contacts on several different levels and the organization of public events in several African capitals, had even broader dimensions. In 2007 , there were direct talks with Lesotho's Justice Minister, M. Mahase, in Maseru, as well as attempts in Mali to secure UN abstentions, including a meeting with President Amadou Toumani Tore aimed at achieving abolition by the end of 2008 and involving religious groups in an effort to gain popular support and organize a front of cultural support for alternative forms of justice. There was a similar effort in Niger, aimed first at obtaining an abstention at the UN and then at getting an abolitionist legislative process underway.

November 15 came. I followed the events at the UN from Sant'Egidio headquarters in Trastevere. I must say that the result was no foregone conclusion, and that the result, immensely favorable, had really been decided only in the last few days, thanks to the combined actions undertaken inside and outside the United Nations. An exceptional role was played by public and private Italians, by the generous and professional officials of states like New Zealand, Italy, and France, as well as the World Coalition.

The Resolution was presented by the ambassador from Gabon, so as to dispel the notion that it was a "white" and a "rich countries'" initiative. All in all, it was a joint effort that found a way of respecting the autonomy of individual countries. It was Italian diplomacy at its best, too, meeting the challenges of credibility, respect, and the ability to work with others, including the Portuguese presidency and all the European and non-European partners.

The United States and China, like India and Japan, chose to keep a low profile.

There was a clamor on the floor, led by Singapore and Egypt as well as some Caribbean countries, like Barbados. They sought to attach "killing amendments" to the bill so that it would not pass. But all of their amendments, written and oral, were defeated.

A last "killing amendment," presented by Egypt, aimed

at binding the abolition of the death penalty to the abolition of abortion. It was a clever move to try to create division among Western countries, touching a sensitive issue. The Philippine ambassador took the floor and said that his country, predominantly Catholic, did not agree with the amendment, since it was not in the agenda of the Resolution. The representative from the Vatican, an observer state, said the Vatican would refuse to countenance any exploitation of the issue of life, or any attempt to decide which life was worth saving. In my opinion, it was a crucial passage. From that moment on there was no more resistance.

When the vote was taken, the outcome was clear: the Resolution had passed decisively in the Third Committee, with ninety-nine member states in favor. This was one more than the simple majority we'd needed, and many more than the fifty-two countries who'd voted against. The United States voted against. China voted against and India voted against. Jamaica and many other Caribbean countries voted against. Egypt voted against. Somalia and Zimbabwe voted against. Afghanistan voted against. Saudi Arabia and Iran voted against. Singapore voted against. North Korea voted against.

The applause and enthusiasm on the floor were commensurate with the resistance that had held up the presentation and approval of such a document for almost fifteen years. Although the Resolution was non-binding, it set an international moral standard, asserting that the death penalty was a question of human rights, not just one of internal justice. Capital punishment became an issue for the international community, and not just the "good souls" at the NGOs. It engaged the United Nations and the Secretary General in the task of monitoring the situation and preparing an annual report on the implementation of the Resolution.

The General Assembly announced that the Resolution would come up for a vote in mid-December. I went to New York again, and on December 18, 2007, I was in the General Assembly Hall with members of the Italian Mission in seats behind the ambassador from the Republic of Italy, Giulio Terzi di Sant'Agata; Massimo D'Alema, the Foreign Affairs minister; and a hard worker at the Italian Mission, Stefano Gatti. Of course, Sergio D'Elia of Hands Off Cain was sitting in the same row.

Hard-line retentionist states, fearing a loss and wanting to minimize the damage, had arranged a small number of speeches followed by a single vote on the whole Resolution rather than a line-by-line vote. The promoter of the Resolution had agreed to it.

The vote was 102 member states in favor, fifty-four against, twenty-nine abstaining, and five absent.

The Resolution had passed, resoundingly, as if this were the most natural thing in the world!

In the intervening weeks, Burundi and Burkina Faso changed their positions to vote in favor of the text. Guinea Conakry, Cameroon, Tanzania, and the Central African

Republic had decided to abstain rather than vote against. Ivory Coast had joined the group of co-sponsors on the last day before the vote. Blaise Compaoré, president of Burkina Faso, had made a pledge to Sant'Egidio that his country would abolish the death penalty as soon as the Resolution was approved (but the plan ran into trouble in the following years, when Compaoré attempted unsuccessfully to extend his presidential term before resigning in October 2014). It should be noted that Sant'Egidio had fostered a first accord to stop the civil war in Ivory Coast, and that later, with the Burkinabé President, had brokered the final peace accord that reunified Ivory Coast after five years. All this turned out to be useful at the decisive moment.

Once again, the United States had voted against the Resolution, and at first the American press seemed to snub the event. A crucial vote on a major human rights issue that is hugely controversial in the United States garnered just fifteen lines in the following day's *New York Times*. Two days later, though, the Gray Lady spoke.

An editorial on the paper's editorial pages—where the editorial line of the *Times* is established—summarized the events under the headline *A Pause from Death*:

> The United States, as usual, lined up on the other side, with Iran, China, Pakistan, Sudan and Iraq. Together this blood brotherhood accounts for more than 90 percent of the

world's executions, according to Amnesty International. These countries' devotion to their sovereignty is rigid, as is their perverse faith in execution as a criminal deterrent and an instrument of civilized justice. But out beyond Texas, Ohio, Virginia, Myanmar, Singapore, Saudi Arabia and Zimbabwe, there are growing numbers who expect better of humanity.

Many are not nations or states but groups of regular people, organizations like the Community of Sant'Egidio, a lay Catholic movement begun in Italy whose advocacy did much to bring about this week's successful vote in the General Assembly.

I cannot speak for others, but I know that the night the Resolution passed was for me a moment of pure happiness—one of the purest such moments in my life. Here was a victory of David over Goliath, except that David was not just one person but many people, working and hoping together. I was just a spokesperson for this entire world of courageous people.

The Resolution for a Moratorium on the Death Penalty has come up in the United Nations several times since then. Each time it has passed, and each time the support for it has been greater than the last. Our hope is that someday support for the abolition of the death penalty will be truly universal.

12.
The Innocents

The Innocence Project, an NGO devoted to the exoneration of people wrongfully convicted, puts it plainly: "These DNA exoneration cases have provided irrefutable proof that wrongful convictions are not isolated or rare events, but arise from systemic defects that can be precisely identified and addressed."

Back in 1992, when the Innocence Project was founded, DNA testing was a new technology, and co-founders Barry Schenk and Peter Neufeld thought that it could be used to prove the innocence of convicted criminals. At the same time, new research was calling into question the reliability of eyewitness testimony. Schenk and Neufeld had worked as public defenders in the Bronx, where they freed a man named Marion Coakley who had been sentenced to fifteen years. Although multiple witnesses, including his priest, supported his alibi, the victim and another person with her at the time of the event stated that she had seen the face of her attacker. Schenk and Neufeld used DNA testing to prove that Coakley was not that attacker, and his conviction was overturned.

Since 1992, the Innocence Project has freed 173 of the 321 people exonerated by DNA testing in the United States. It is a founding member of the Innocence Network, an affiliation of more than sixty-two independent organizations dedicated to overturning wrongful convictions and improving the criminal justice system. Among other successes, the Innocence Project has helped to reform eyewitness identification procedures to reduce the rate of misidentification in a number of states, including New Jersey, Ohio and North Carolina, and in major cities including Boston, Minneapolis, Dallas ,and others, and helped prisoners with claims of innocence to apply for post-conviction DNA testing in all fifty states.

◄◦►

Why do wrongful convictions happen? And how often do they happen?

Across the world, the death penalty is used to target political opposition and religious and social minorities. In South Korea in recent decades, two former presidents have been sentenced to death, political retribution by their successors after power changed hands. It happens to presidents, but much more often to ordinary people. Governments rely on a lack of reporting of these cases, as well as the typically poor quality of public legal defense and a lack of expertise in death penalty jurisprudence on the part of both defense lawyers and the judges. When the accused is poor, the chances of a wrongful conviction soar!

In the United States, a sophisticated and strong democracy in so many ways, wrongful execution is not a rare event, but a "systemic problem."

I have spoken with wardens, officials, people sentenced to death, relatives of victims and of convicts, police officers and observers, chaplains and spiritual advisers on death row, people in charge of the system, and human rights activists. I have asked them all how many of the people on death row might, in their opinions, be innocent. Their answers have led me to conclude that as many as one out of seven people who are executed did not commit the crime for which they were sentenced to death.

"I am sorry." It is the first thought that comes into your mind when you meet someone who has spent years on death row and is simply innocent.

Whenever I meet a person who has spent a significant part of his or her life on death row, I try to say something like this, simple and true and sympathetic: "I am sorry for what happened to you."

And every time I get a strange glance and something like the same answer:

"Why?"

"I am a blessed human being."

"I am alive."

"I have understood a lot of things about life."

As Nick Yarris put it to me while walking down the center aisle of the Basilica of Santa Maria in Trastevere after our prayer service one evening, "I was an asshole, a jerk. I am not one now."

Nicholas Yarris—Nick—is very direct, not ashamed of anything. Tall, bald, and still handsome (he showed me pictures of himself with black hair, pictures from his life "before"), he speaks slowly and calmly, without drama, even if tears well up in his eyes. But I can't forget the evening of the Cities for Life World Day at the Coliseum. Afterwards, there were five or six of us walking back along the *Via dei Fori Imperiali,* a road that cuts the Roman Forum in two through what may be the most interesting archaeological area in the world, towards the *Piazza Venezia*, a sort of crossroads at Rome's historical center. We were all walking side by side, but Nick was walking backwards. Sometimes he was taking pictures, other times just walking—but backwards. It was a little strange, but none of us said anything about it. *I have no right to judge,* I said to myself, *because there is so much suffering behind it.* Then Nick spoke up, as if answering the unspoken questions in our minds. "Do you think it's strange? That I'm a strange guy? I haven't seen such a moon for twenty-two years, haven't seen this wide, infinite sky with stars, or this air. And the Coliseum all lit up. I don't want to miss one second of this. That's why I'm walking backwards . . ."

Nick spent 8,057 days on death row, and he read about six thousand books—one every day or two. The rest of the time he tried to keep from being killed by the State of Pennsylvania.

Another friend of mine, Mario Flores, who spent twenty years on death row in Illinois, says that he doesn't remember how many books he read there: maybe sixty or seventy-five, books about religion, God, and art mostly—"Italian Renaissance art, and Diego Rivera, Frida Kahlo, the Mexican surrealist."

These two innocents are very different cases. Yarris was a drug user. Flores was a top young athlete from a Mexican-American family in Chicago, who was on track to represent Mexico in diving at the Olympics (and whom his family wanted out of bad circles). He was a ladies' man who had one foot in the gang culture of Chicago's poor neighborhoods and the other in the more elevated circles of the school his family had made sacrifices to send him to.

Nick Yarris was arrested on Dec 20, 1981, miles away from the scene of the rape and murder of Linda Craig, who had been kidnapped five days earlier in the parking lot of the Tri State Mall in Delaware, near the border with Pennsylvania. Nick was stopped for a traffic violation; but he was high on methamphetamine, and by the end of that day he was in a Delaware county jail. Bail was set at $100,000.

Mario Flores was charged in November 1984 for a crime that had been committed eleven months earlier, in the early hours of New Year's Day. Mario was at a New Year's Eve party at the time, and many witnesses placed him there. But he had loaned his car for the night to two alleged co-conspirators who both testified against Mario and thus obtained immunity from prosecution for themselves. According to the testimony, Mario and two companions were driving in Chicago at 2 AM on January 1, 1984, when they pulled over at the scene of a bad car accident and found a man and a woman in a heated argument about the collision. Supposedly, Mario and his companions stepped in to defend the woman, and the man then threatened Mario and the woman. He told them that he belonged to a notorious street gang, and went to his car to get a gun. According to the testimony, Mario then shot the man several times, killing him, and one of his companions stole a necklace from the deceased after the attack. Despite his alibi, Mario was charged with murder in the course of an armed robbery, a crime then punishable by death in Illinois.

Nick's case, as he relates in the book he wrote from death row, shows how one can get drawn into the world of capital punishment for absurd reasons. It can happen to anyone. Nick was thrown in jail. After a week in jail—a week of "cold turkey" withdrawal from methamphetamines—he tried to hang himself, but was stopped. A few days later he read about Linda Craig's death in a newspaper that he found in the jail, and although he knew nothing about it, he figured that if he made up a story about the crime and gave it to the police they would let him go. So he invented one about a drug buddy of his doing the killing, a man he thought had died from a drug overdose. But it turned out the man was alive, and disproved Nick's story.

Now the police turned on Nick and pressured him into confessing the crime himself. It was winter. They made him strip to his boxer shorts, settled him on a mattress, and turned a group of gang members on him. "I was verbally abused, pissed on, covered with freezing water, for days. This was how it started," Nick explains. Then he was charged with the abduction, rape, and murder of Linda Craig. He had a receipt that showed he was in a store twenty miles from the scene the night the crime took place, and the store's owner remembered seeing him there. But those pieces of hard evidence were not enough.

The blood on the victim's clothing was tested for blood group, sub-group, and secretor status. From this test, the prosecution concluded that the murderer had type B-positive blood and a B-positive secretor as well. As it happens, Nick Yarris is B-positive. So is 15 percent of the world's male population. So was Linda Craig's husband. And because she and he were unable to have children, they had no reason to use contraception, meaning that the semen found inside her after the rape could well have been his. Even so, Nick was convicted and sentenced to death in 1982.

Mario was nineteen years old when he found himself

living in a windowless cell ten feet square for a crime that had nothing to do with him. He had had the support of his family and that was key. They'd sold their house to pay for his legal expenses. Once in prison, Mario studied law by correspondence course and became a licensed legal assistant. He started to defend himself and some of his fellow death row inmates, in four instances helping them get off death row. And he became an accomplished painter, a real artist. Instead of going to the Olympics, he went to Illinois's death row, where he dove into colors. He had to find a way not to become crazy—to fight and, somehow, to win. "Painting saved my life," he told me. "I started to create the world I was living in, to make the walls of my cell disappear."

Two years after he was convicted, Nick considered killing himself again, this time with a razor blade. He failed, and that's when he decided to fight his wrongful conviction, that he would not rest until every angle had been tried. He decided that he could not cause any more pain to his family. "My oldest brother suffered brain damage in an accident when he was eighteen and became an alcoholic," Nick told me. "My youngest brother died of an overdose. I was a drug addict myself. Why add to the pain? Why become, as they said I was, a killer, of myself or of other people, someone enslaved by rage? So I decided just to become a man, a different man, a good man. For my parents, for myself."

A DNA test would have exonerated Nick from the

beginning, but in 1982 these tests were primitive and rarely performed. He was convicted and—because the combination of rape, abduction, and murder suggested an extraordinary level of malice—sentenced to death.

Nick first learned of the exonerating potential of DNA in the *Philadelphia Inquirer* on March 20, 1988—after six years on death row. Through his lawyer at the time, Joseph Bullen, he asked for DNA analysis of the evidence in his own case. Due to the loss or destruction of a great deal of the evidence, and due to the state's repeated refusal to examine other slides related to the case, it took more than fifteen years for Nick to obtain the results that led to his exoneration.

Nick became the first death row prisoner in Pennsylvania to be discharged by a DNA test.

Nick and Mario each spent more than twenty years on death row, although neither of them had had anything to do with the crime of which he was convicted, or even been near the crime scene.

—◦—

"I thought of suicide almost every day," Bill Nieves told me. Nieves was an innocent man who was wrongfully convicted and sentenced to death in Pennsylvania, where he spent six years on death row. In 2000 he was exonerated after a retrial—the eighty-seventh person in the US to be exonerated by DNA evidence.

"The most difficult thing is not to accept yourself as the sub-human the system tells you you are every day on death row. In prison, everything around you says that: the shouting, the violence, the low pay for your work, and having to pay a lot of money simply to get treated when you are sick—often getting the wrong treatment. It is natural for the system to do that. Once it's agreed that you are an animal, a sub-human, the system has no problems getting rid of you when the time comes, sees no contradiction in human beings doing this to you as a sub-human, and no reason to be humane."

Bill Nieves was convicted of capital murder in 1994, but was released after a new trial in 2000. Compared to Nick, he was lucky. "I know I couldn't believe it when I received a call from my lawyer saying, 'They've agreed to a retrial,' and I couldn't believe the happiness of the other people on death row for me, of the other sub-humans when they heard me shouting, 'Retrial!'"

I asked him, "How did you feel and what did you do on the first day after your release? "

"I went to my relatives' place. There was a sofa in the living room for me. That night I didn't sleep. Not one minute all through the night. Every once in a while I got up and went to the door and turned the handle to check that it wasn't locked. I knew it wasn't. But I couldn't believe it. I did that all night long."

About the appeals process, Nieves has this to say: "To those of you who believe that the appeals courts weed out unconstitutional convictions, and/or look for instances where someone is saying, `Hey, I can prove my innocence,' you believe wrongly. The state courts are interested in protecting convictions. The federal court is left to weed through the morass of deceit on either side as appeals proceed. Period."

Nick Yarris confirmed this. "Starting in 1988," Nick explained, "I fought to get a court, any court, to listen to me about how I had uncovered facts that showed I could not have committed the crime. Not a day, not a single day went by that I wasn't pushing to get my case heard. I even filed a federal lawsuit trying to force the state court to hear my claims."

The court told him he had missed a deadline. "Here I was, a man fighting to be heard, and in the end, this justice, speaking on behalf of the Supreme Court of Pennsylvania, said I should have filed my claims earlier, even though [earlier] this same court had invited me to file it later. To tell me that I hadn't filed in time was plainly vicious."

In Pennsylvania, the standard incarceration for death row inmates is solitary confinement. Nick spent twenty-two years in solitary, fourteen without touching another person except for the times he was beaten after breaking the rules. In 2003, Nick's appeals had been exhausted. He was exhausted. He had given up. He wrote a letter to the governor asking to be executed.

But around the same time there were also new

glimmers of light. Dr. Mohammed Tahir, a forensic expert from Indianapolis, joined Dr. Edward Blake of Forensic Science Associates in California to help with the DNA testing in Nick's case. Results began pouring in. "Nothing was matching me, on the gloves, on the underwear of the poor victim. Nothing," Nick says.

Nick was exonerated. But he was not yet a free man — his sentence had been compounded as punishment for an attempted escape and crimes committed in flight. "I had to demonstrate that if I had not been a victim of wrongful conviction I would have not committed the crime of trying to escape and those connected to it. The irony is that I had to serve about five more weeks in prison. The guards did not know what to do with me." In the end, a Florida judge ruled that all the crimes Nick had been charged with merited a prison sentence of seventeen years—precisely the time he had already served.

Now I understand what Nick said to me that night after the prayer service. "I have no time to be unhappy. I cannot let them take away my life now that I am once again a human being. I have no time to be angry."

He has only one regret: not doing enough for those who are still on death row. It angers him that there is so little interest in making sure the evidence in capital cases is sound, or in finding the real perpetrators of crimes.

Nick is married, and he and his wife, Karen, have a beautiful daughter. They live in London. After winning his freedom, Nick—who was homeless following his release from prison—received a four million dollar settlement from the Commonwealth of Pennsylvania. In this he is a rare exception. Many states, before releasing a prisoner—even one who has been exonerated—require a declaration that they will never be asked for any financial compensation.

"Now I have all the world to live in," Nick says. "And I have the responsibility to live not just for myself."

—◦—

Mario Flores too is in love with a beautiful woman. But he has not been given the satisfaction of a complete acquittal.

In 2003, Governor George Ryan was ready to announce the commutation of all death sentences in Illinois to life sentences, and also to admit that some death penalty convictions were not based on solid evidence. "My lawyers and I were told that he would give the final announcement of my wrongful conviction. But we waited and waited, and the press conference never happened. It was too risky to wait any longer. We accepted a commutation of the death sentence to forty years, admitting the crime that I had never committed but had been charged with. I had served for twenty years on death row. After serving half of the days of my sentence in prison, by law I could go out. Which I did."

On the outside, Mario was treated as an undesirable,

despite his innocence. By birth, he was a Mexican citizen, and although he had never lived in that country, the US government deported him there.

Mario lives in Mexico City, "where I am scared for my wife, since there is a lot of violence and she is so kind and beautiful." He is now a painter, and his art is exhibited all over the world.

"I am not Leonardo, I am not Raphael," he says. "But I love classical beauty and how it mingles with my pre-Columbian blood and origins, Maya blood that pulses with the need of liberation. I can be a man who has a lot to live for and to give others, a man who has started to live again at forty. To live for my family who never abandoned me. And for the friends I have found afterward. And for my children. And to end the death penalty."

—◦—

In the beginning there were Barry Scheck and Peter Neufel, co-founders of the Innocence Project. Now there are hundreds of lawyers and activists and groups devoted to reversing wrongful convictions.

And there is a flip side of the exoneration process, which is that it makes it possible to identify the true perpetrators of crimes. Of the 321 post-conviction DNA exonerations in the United States, twenty were of people sentenced to death. About 70 percent are people of color. In 50 percent of cases the real perpetrator was identified thanks to DNA tests. And 60 percent of the wrongfully convicted have been compensated financially. Exonerations have been won in thirty-eight US states and in Washington, DC.

The fact that eyewitness misidentification is the single greatest cause of wrongful convictions in America, the basis of 72 percent of convictions overturned through DNA testing, should make each of us consider the necessity of re-thinking the whole system and abolishing "the ultimate punishment," the only irreversible penalty. In at least 30 percent of these cases, there were signed confessions too. We often associate eyewitnesses and confessions with high levels of certainty, but we're wrong.

In all this, it's worth keeping in mind that the perfect justice system does not exist. This alone is a reason to abolish the death penalty. Nobody should be empowered by the state to take away something that cannot be given back if it turns out that a mistake was made. And if what was taken is life itself?

13.
Thirteen Ways to Live Without the Death Penalty

We can look at the death penalty every which way, but it is always a travesty, even when it is not being used for reasons that are obviously unjust—to eliminate enemies, rivals, or unpopular beliefs; to maintain a leader's hold on power; to dehumanize a group of people. Even when the death penalty is used for the supposedly civilized reasons of public safety and deterrence, or when its goal is simple retribution, even when its aims are modest, capital punishment fails to achieve them.

We cannot create new life by imposing death. Justice that kills is never justice. Justice implies at its roots the responsibility to save life, every life. When this principle is lost, justice enters into conflict with itself. Every execution adds death to death and creates unrecoverable loss, compounding victimhood with victimhood. It ratifies the worst that has already happened by multiplying its destructive effect, prolonging it in time and involving others. It is a defeat for life, a victory for death.

So what should we do instead? We should work for the victory of life over death.

Specifically, we should work to abolish the death penalty. But how? Here are thirteen ways of joining life row.

1.

Work to ensure that your government has a constitution that prohibits the death penalty altogether.

Ninety-seven countries have abolished the death penalty. Short of full abolition, dozens of countries whose populaces are still divided over capital punishment have at least abolished it for lesser crimes like theft, and another eight countries have abolished it for "ordinary crimes" while keeping it available under military law.

2.

Work to bring about a moratorium on executions, whether by law or in practice.

A moratorium is a written commitment on the part of a government to forgo the practice of capital punishment, leaving aside broader questions of whether the death penalty can ever be useful or effective. As it falls short of a constitutional ban, a moratorium is something of a partial measure. Still, the patchwork of nations that have enacted moratoria on executions or more partial bans on the death penalty totals nearly 150—about three-quarters of the world where capital punishment is not practiced.

3.
Create support for the human rights protocol now gaining momentum worldwide.

As of late 2014, eighty-one countries had signed the Second Optional Protocol to the International Covenant on Civil and Political Rights (ICCPR). Once ratified by a nation's parliament, this protocol binds that nation not to allow anyone under its jurisdiction to be executed.

150 countries have to ratify the Protocol before it can take effect. With only eighty-one signatories so far, we have a long way to go. This is another way to work for the abolition of the death penalty: by applying pressure on individual governments to ratify the Protocol. An international association of MPs opposed to the death penalty associated with Parliamentarians for Global Action (PGA) is taking shape, and this body could be an effective tool, because parliamentarians can influence their peers in government, so that those who are already working to promote the Protocol in retentionist countries do not feel as isolated.

4.
Show how the death penalty actually works— and doesn't work.

This one is easy—because there is a huge mass of evidence demonstrating that the death penalty doesn't work. The thing to do is to put all that information to good use.

Develop studies on the ground. Show how prevalent the death penalty is in certain places. Illustrate how ineffectual it is in reducing prison costs and deterring further crimes. Demonstrate how disproportionately it affects poor people, people of color, immigrants, undocumented citizens, and people with intellectual disabilities. Point out how few capital cases actually result in executions, noting the cost of capital prisoners' prolonged incarceration and appeals process. Emphasize how many death sentences are based on corrupt or insufficient evidence, murky or contradictory eyewitness testimony, or jailhouse plea bargains.

5.
Talk to your friends, your parents, your children.

Much of the information that I present in this short book has not been widely available before. Talk to people. Share. You'll be amazed at how receptive most people are to opening up this dark corner of our world and letting light and air in. Talk to lawyers, bar associations, teachers, journalists, and opinion makers.

6.
Work to advance the understanding that freedom from death is a basic and universal human right.

The concept of a "universal human right" may sound

abstract, but this is an approach that is much more useful and practical than it sounds—in Africa, especially. And even in the US it is a useful formulation, one that people can benefit from hearing more often than they do now.

The Organization of American States requires that all member states implement the American Convention on Human Rights, which explicitly forbids the reinstatement of the death penalty by any member country and has a specific protocol calling for its abolition. Now the African Union is working toward something similar: a resolution modeled on the UN General Assembly Resolution that calls for a "moratorium on the use of the death penalty."

This can be an effective pursuit for international and local activists alike. In the European Union, the process already has a natural ally in the Council of Europe. The European Convention on Human Rights forbids the death penalty in all circumstances. Any state that wishes to be a party to this convention must implement Protocols 6 and 13, which uncompromisingly demand abolition. And in this way, through the language of international amity and cooperation, the nations of the world create and bind themselves to a culture of life row.

7.
Work to abolish the death penalty within yourself.

We can help abolish the death penalty by starting with ourselves—by working to reduce our level of anger, our habits of retaliation, and our fear that we will not be taken seriously if we don't marshal all the resources of will and control available to us.

Retaliation is a shortcut that political leaders often take—and one that the citizens of the world will one day refuse. We can all play a role in bringing this about by refusing to take retaliatory postures in our own lives, even when we are wronged, and thus overcoming habits of revenge.

8.

Accept that there is nothing wrong with
allowing ourselves to be vulnerable.

Just as we are taught to hold back from sharing the pain of others, so too we are taught to believe that if we have too many deep feelings of our own we'll wind up feeling too much pain. The fear of being hurt in our relationships often wins out over the chance to live through our relationships.

We all strive for simplicity. But oversimplification is not the solution.

Create a life row where a death row was.

9.

Work to create a society that is not
enslaved to revenge and fear.

In the West, recent decades especially have been marked by a culture of fear. Fear of terrorist attacks, of street crime, of the unexpected ups and downs of the economy, and fear of not knowing who we are. In a global and interconnected world, many live in a state of true disorientation: no homeland, no knowledge of one's roots, no control over one's political environment.

To live with the death penalty is to live under the illusion that if we as a society find an enemy and dispel it, fear will disappear from our lives and we will feel at home in the world. Unfortunately, the opposite is the case: we look for enemies because we do not know, too often, who we are, how we want to live, and where we want to go. In times of uncertainty everyone can become an enemy. Those on death row give expression to our barely suppressed wish to do away with them all.

The alternative is to live without fear—even without fear of senseless death.

Revenge is always distance. But we know that love can never be death, it can only mean life.

Anyone can defeat that special kind of disease that aims to create a society of dumb people, people who cannot be touched by anything, who are not ready to fight for the people they love when the time comes.

If there is a creed that unites many of us in the world today, it is individualism. But the deeper truth is that no man or woman is an island.

10.

Recognize that the death penalty has not made us any
safer and that no one executed by the state can be said to
have "gotten what they deserved."

To envision a world without the death penalty is to
work for a safer world. It starts, simply enough, with the
recognition that things are never black and white, that
no party to any dispute has a monopoly on good or evil.
Whatever may have happened, whatever crimes may
have been committed, there is humanity on death row—
decent people who know human weakness, who feel
compassion for their victims and sorrow for what they
or others did. There are even, perhaps, saints, who after a
long pilgrimage towards awareness and purification have
come to know the hell their acts have created for other
people.

11.

Try to identify with the victims of the death
penalty as an act of compassion.

People in prison live lives that are extraordinary in their
lacks and absences: no natural light, no liberty, no human
companionship, no difference between one day and the
next, no right to live free from fear and violence. Many
succumb to the trials of prison life. Many others become
better people than they were before. Death row is a place

where one is inevitably and profoundly changed: either dehumanized or enriched and refined in humanity.

We can learn that the right way to demonstrate our grief for a murdered loved one is not anger and hatred. That is a trap. Many people fear that if they do not hate the person who murdered their spouse, brother, sister, or friend, they haven't shown love for their beloved. That is never true.

Compassion is never a lack of strength. Instead, it is strength expressed at its highest, least primitive level.

12.
*Start corresponding with a person on death row,
their relatives, and relatives of their victims.*

Individual people can do it; school and church groups can do it; neighborhoods and towns can do it. You can be pen pals with a death row prisoner, with a death row prisoner's relatives, or with the relatives of victims. However it comes about, such correspondence builds a bridge between two worlds that generally do not communicate. For a person on death row, friendship with a free person is a window to the world outside. Often the correspondent becomes like a brother or sister, the family the prisoner never had.

Once the letters are going back and forth, consider it an opportunity to set aside or overcome all the differences in power and freedom between the two of you. The person on death row will remember every word, every crumb of human candor, while our own lives are so full that we hardly pay attention to the details of them. In this way both partners can grow.

We can also befriend and empathize with the families of both death row prisoners and their victims. This is perhaps the darkest and most neglected side of the death penalty.

The quality of prison life is a test of civilization for a whole society. A society that does not hide its sick, its old, and even its guilty is a society that is less afraid of sickness, old age, and criminality; lives *in extremis* become reminders of how various life is.

13.
Join together with others; ask one another,
what can be done that hasn't already been done?

There are nearly as many ways of resisting the death penalty and its culture of revenge as there are people. In contemplating forms of resistance, you may find a way that nobody else has tried before.

Many NGOs are internationally active in trying to envision ways of resisting the death penalty: Amnesty International, Death Penalty Focus, Hands Off Cain, the Community of Sant'Egidio, Together Against the Death Penalty, Texas Coalition, Great Caribbean for Life, Murders' Victims Families for Human Rights, and Journey of Hope, to name a few.

In a campaign like the one against capital punishment, it's always better to create a network of activists with whom we can share hopes, labor, and commitment—whether two or three friends, a group of local people, or an international movement. That's the reason to mark the World Day Against the Death Penalty on October 10, and on November 30 to support the Cities for Life, Cities Against the Death Penalty movement.

You can help build a consensus behind the UN resolution against the death penalty; you can put pressure on your government to implement it, using the recommendations contained in the Secretary General's biennial Report as a tool. You can urge your elected leaders to promote the ratification of binding treaties such as the Second Optional Protocol to the International Covenant on Civil and Political rights. And while you do, remember: nothing is impossible.

Give this book as a gift to someone you care about. Contact the publisher to inquire about discounts on bulk purchases. If you or someone you love is a prisoner, write to the publisher for a free copy.

A world without the death penalty: it *is* possible. And we can see it. It is happening already.

Afterword
Paul Elie

To understand the death penalty, Mario Marazziti likes to say, you have to go to Texas. In 2000 (having seen San Quentin in California) he went to Texas, and that has made all the difference. After that trip, and through many more, came his friendships with John Paul Penry, Dominique Green, Eddie Johnson and other men sentenced to death. After it came the World Coalition for the Death Penalty, the moratoria on executions in individual countries, the presentation of 3.2 million signatures to the United Nations Secretary General, the UN General Assembly's statement against the inhumanity of capital punishment, and the pledges of several dozen countries to abolish the death penalty or suspend its use. Out of that trip, that is, came the growing movement for abolition of the death penalty worldwide; and out of it came the thirteen ways of looking at the death penalty presented in this book.

Just as Mario had to go to Texas to understand the death penalty, if we want to understand the present movement against the death penalty we have to go to Trastevere. In Trastevere—the rustic, vibrant district "across the Tiber" from imperial Rome—the group of friends known as the Community of Sant'Egidio came together in the spring of 1968 and began their efforts, first in the *periferia*, Rome's outskirts, then Southern Italy, Northern Europe, Africa, and now overlooked or disdained places and peoples all over the world. In Trastevere they developed an informal way of working together rooted in friendship rather than authority or efficiency, and made it a new model for activism akin to the ones developed in Velvet Revolution Prague, Zuccotti Park, and Tahrir Square. In Trastevere they brought together rival tribes and hard-line Marxist-Leninists from Mozambique to settle a bloody civil war through dialogue and what they call "weak strength"—an approach that, when you see it in practice, really makes you think that friendship can change the world.

The guidebooks still call Trastevere a working-class district, and so it is in some respects. There are still plenty of working people in its walk-up flats and apartment houses. Yet the district—a short walk across the bridge from the Campo de' Fiori, a stroll along the pilgrim path from St. Peter's Basilica—has lately become an upscale bohemia akin to the East Village or the Mission District. The ochre apartments (and the people stepping out of them) are a feast for the eye, and an actual feast is available on every corner, from the *trattorie* Fellini frequented to the posh and modern Glass to the floating Irish pub moored in the river. In summertime, especially, it can seem that the carnival of food and drink, of fashion shoots and artisanal this-and-that, has shoved the place once celebrated as "Rome for Romans" aside.

On the face of it, Trastevere is a postreligious place, too. Churches are everywhere, it's true, and the *trasteverini* regard St. Francis of Assisi (who stayed there while in Rome) and Raphael (who called on his mistress, the Fornarina, there) as native sons. And yet most churches are closed most days, shuttered, chained up, and implacable, so that they strike you not as destinations or even as buildings but as outcroppings on the landscape.

But there's one significant exception. In early evening, crowds of people converge on the piazza fronting on the Basilica of Santa Maria in Trastevere, whose bell tower is the local landmark. They are on their way to eat at one of the four hundred local restaurants, to smoke a cigarette or lick a gelato near the old stone fountain, to watch mimes and acrobats perform in the piazza. Or they are actually bound for the basilica itself, where, at 8:30 every weeknight, Sant'Egidio holds the nightly service known as *la preghiera*.

I have been to the service perhaps a dozen times. You pick up a book and a headset and find a seat on a long bench below the ancient mosaics of Christ, a tallish proto-modern Mary, and the earliest Roman saints. The church—it must hold a little more than a thousand people—is full or nearly so. The crowd is mixed: young and old, stylish and not, lay and clerical, Italian and German and African. An organ note is struck and the call and response begins. There's a recitation of the Litany of the Saints (the ancient names read off and invoked) and a reading from the New or Old Testament. A member of the community gives a homily in Italian, which can be heard in simultaneous translation on the headset. Then comes the *Padre Nostro*—the Lord's Prayer. This is not a Mass (that is on Saturday night). There is no Communion, and, generally, no priest presiding, and so it ends abruptly, with people spilling out of the basilica, already in conversation, and into the square.

They aren't leaving, though. They are in the middle of things. Many of them have come to *la preghiera* after putting in a day's effort at one of the Sant'Egidio projects scattered through Trastevere. Behind a plain door on a steep hill, the Community's pantry feeds 1,200 poor people a three-course meal, with Sant'Egidio members acting as waiters. A flat nearby is the office of the Community's adoption service, which makes matches between European couples and children from Cambodia, Burkina Faso, and other countries. A back street near where Francis of Assisi worshiped among lepers is a welcome center for Gypsies and immigrants, and homeless Italians as well, who find hot showers, clean clothes, help in avoiding deportation, leads on jobs, or just a place to sit down and be known by name. On the Piazza Sant'Egidio behind the basilica is the Trattoria gli Amici, which employs mentally disabled men and women as maitres d', waiters, cooks, and sommeliers—and so has created new jobs for people with special talents at a time when, in Italy, a good job is hard to come by. Every Christmas Day, the Community makes the basilica of Santa Maria itself a space of welcome for several thousand of Rome's poor people—Italian as well as Mexican, Peruvian, African, Syrian—who are invited to eat a holiday meal on red-draped tables set up on the priceless Cosmati tile floor in the nave.

It's a paradox: this sixteen-hundred-year-old church, the oldest church in the world consecrated to the Virgin Mary, built on the site where the Roman Christians to whom St. Paul addressed his letter met for their prayer service—this most ancient of Rome's still-standing basilicas is also the least museum-like of them all. It's a meeting place, a social hub, a bazaar of ideas and good works, and a hothouse of conviviality, where strangers become friends and friends become more than friends.

—◦—

One evening a few years ago I met Mario Marazziti in the rear of Santa Maria after *la preghiera* and we set out for supper at a favorite place of his, making our way through the crowd of people outside the church—with whom we had been invoking the saints a few minutes earlier—and down one of the narrow streets leading from the piazza to the Tiber. An early member of the Community, Mario gradually stepped into the role of its volunteer *portavoce,* or spokesman. When I first met him, in 1998, he was employed as a TV producer and manager for RAI, Italy's state media company, and I was writing a piece about Catholic-Jewish relations for the *New York Times Magazine*. I'm not sure what I expected in a humanitarian from RAI, but I didn't expect Mario, whose dark suit, straight black hair, and big smile seemed to suggest an Italian ex-Beatle.

If Trastevere embodies the paradox of Europe—emphatically old but with pockets of exceptional vitality—Mario Marazziti embodies the paradox of Sant'Egidio: at once wholly worldly and something like holy. Or so I have come to feel as I've gotten to know him across fifteen years. He is no stranger to high society: through an old friend at the prominent wine journal *Gambero Rosso* he and his friends put together Vino per Vita, or Wine for Life, an initiative where Italian wineries run by Mario's contacts give the proceeds from certain bottlings to Sant'Egidio's campaign for AIDS relief in Africa. He can be irreverent, relishing the story of a cleric friend whose poor Italian led him to open the church's millennial ceremonies in 1999 with a crude profanity. For years, he spent part of each New York visit hunting down audio gear for his son, Andrea, a rock guitarist. Yet he is selfless and tireless on behalf of Sant'Egidio—on behalf, he says, of "the gospel and friendship." I had learned of him through a Sant'Egidio group at St. Malachy's Church near Times Square led by the author Thomas Cahill, who was hard at work on the third book of his seven-volume "Hinges of History" series. The group never had more than ten members, but Mario sustained us with phone calls and email messages. I later asked him how he kept up with us and his countless other friends worldwide. "Friendship is not proportionate," he said matter-of-factly.

It would be nice to say that over soup and red wine in Trastevere that night Mario told me the story of Sant'Egidio. And why shouldn't he have? There is nobody better able than he, with his years as *portavoce*. And it is a story full of hooks for a journalist in a hurry: civil wars and AIDS relief, presidents and popes, headlines and peace prizes, and dialogue between religious leaders—Catholic, Protestant, Orthodox, Jewish, Muslim.

There is plenty of material in the Community's press kit. But over soup and red wine that night, and on many a night since, Mario told me the stories not of the projects he had undertaken over many years, but those he was engaged in that very week. He explained that he was just back from Mozambique, the base of Sant'Egidio's anti-AIDS program, DREAM, which is overseen by his wife, Cristina, a medical doctor. "From Mozambique and Texas," he corrected himself, and added, "From the culture of life, and the culture of death." In Texas he had visited his friends on death row. And he had made a strange discovery. "The former execution chamber at the prison in Huntsville, the death chamber with the chair, is now a museum of the death penalty in Texas," he said in amazement. "A museum which has an actual curator! Where the old death chair is kept on display!"

As he refilled our glasses from the bottle—a robust red wine from the Sicilian vintner Planeta, the neck of it stickered with an image of a dove crossing a rainbow, Sant'Egidio's logo, indicating participation in the Community's Wine for Life program—I tried to picture him at a Motel 6 in Huntsville, Texas, and to imagine what his friendship might mean to a man sentenced to death.

What it would mean, in the months to follow, was this. Mario would make a documentary for RAI about Texas's death row, called *Thou Shalt not Kill*. He and Tom Cahill would join his friends on death row in a "book group" with Archbishop Desmond Tutu, whose book *No Future Without Forgiveness* Cahill had published during his years as the head of Doubleday's Image Books imprint. He would describe life in the prison at conferences across Europe. As the date drew near for the execution of Dominique Green, whose conviction and sentence of death seemed especially dubious, he would take part in a vigil in Rome, so that in the hours before Green was executed, while the Catholic churches even in Texas paid scant attention to Green's plight, several hundred members of Sant'Egidio were there at Santa Maria in Trastevere, keeping him in their minds and hearts. He would manage to get John Turturro to narrate an English-language version of the film about Green, called *Dominique's Story*. He would present 3.2 million signatures calling for a moratorium on executions to UN Secretary General

Kofi Annan—and would be written up in the *New York Times* as a man "who has used up all his vacation time traveling for the death penalty moratorium." After Silvio Berlusconi was ousted from Italy's premiership once and for all and placed under house arrest, Mario would enter electoral politics—one of the leaders of the 1968 generation whom the center-left drafted to run for office in the hope of repairing Italian politics, run Vegas-style by Berlusconi for most of their adult lives. He would be elected to the lower House of Parliament, the *Camera dei Deputati*. Now when he came to New York, it would be as the head of the Human Rights Committee of the Camera dei Deputati, part of the Italian delegation to the UN General Assembly's "Presidents' Week."

And he would write this book, in English, out of the conviction that the place where the death penalty is most vulnerable just now, is the United States of America.

—◦—

Over time—and many coffees and *cornetti*—the history of the community did emerge in conversation. It's the story of a lay-led, forward-looking Catholic group that has grown and thrived while keeping its simple student ideals in sight. Sant'Egidio is at once one of the church's so-called "new movements," a counterpart to NGOs like Doctors Without Borders and Human Rights Watch, and a peacemaking outfit that has helped end conflicts in Ivory Coast and Guatemala and has pioneered the "preventive peace process" in Guinea and Niger. And yet it remains, for all that, a group of friends—friends who often wear the tapered suits and hand-stitched shoes of Italy's professional class, and who are as apt to sit for a coffee with a homeless person as with an archbishop or the Mayor of Rome.

The movement's founder, Andrea Riccardi, has as a distant ancestor a monk who was beatified, the third of four steps toward being declared a saint. But his own father was a banker, and when he first read the New Testament in earnest it was as a humanities text at the Liceo Virgilio in central Rome. He felt the text was urging him to lead "a more authentic life." He organized a prayer meeting at a nearby church, attracting a dozen students, who set about working among the poor people living on Rome's ragged outskirts. The meeting spread to other high schools in Rome. When the participants entered the Roman university *La Sapienza*, their meetings grew further. After classes they would set out for the *periferia* on their Vespas, and find there, among people on the margins, a new kind of family.

1968, the year of student uprisings, was also high season for activism inspired by the Second Vatican Council, as Catholics worldwide sought to put the "spirit of the Council" into action. But the Community's first members, as they tell it now, had no great inspiration. They were Romans who sought to break through the spirit-killing anonymity of the postwar city. Their texts were the newspaper and the New Testament, their program was "the gospel and friendship," and their models were local heroes: Francis of Assisi; St. Philip Neri, the sixteenth-century city priest, whose home church, the Chiesa Nuova, was the site of their first meetings; and Pier Paolo Pasolini, the eccentrically spiritual Italian filmmaker, who described the *periferia* as "the true face of Rome."

In 1970, when Mario joined the group, the friends who had met at the Chiesa Nuova were still teenagers. As other student movements foundered, theirs grew stronger. Three years later the cardinal of Rome gave them the keys to the disused church of Sant'Egidio, tucked behind the basilica of Santa Maria in Trastevere. The attached convent was owned by the state. The community started to use the abandoned spaces: they were squatters for good causes. The Jesuit scholar Carlo Maria Martini paid a visit, and asked to join their work with the poor in the *periferia*. Soon bishops and cardinals were coming over from a Vatican-owned palazzo round the corner. In those days Sant'Egidio was the only church in central Rome that was open at night, and the prayer service outgrew the tiny church and migrated to the basilica, where it attracted pilgrims from around the world, who in turn founded Sant'Egidio communities of their own.

They kept up their work on Rome's *periferia*, and this led them to the city's center. Upon his election as pope,

John Paul II—the first non-Italian to hold that office since 1523—resolved to make himself known in Rome by paying pastoral calls on all the city's parish churches. During his first visit to a church in Garbatella in outer Rome in December 1978, he met some members of Sant'Egidio and was taken with their approach; he reached out to the group, beginning a relationship that led him, in 1986, to grant Sant'Egidio a charter as a "public lay association."

On Sunday, October 27, 1986, a hundred or so leaders of the world's religions met in Italy to pray for peace. Catholic, Protestant, Orthodox; Jewish and Muslim; Buddhist, Shinto, Hindu; animist and Native American, they made their way up the hill to Assisi, fabled hometown of St. Francis and his friends. After praying in groups at sites around the village, they took turns offering prayers from a stage outside the basilica. As a finale, they went onstage all together: the Orthodox Supreme Patriarch and the Archbishop of Canterbury to the right, the Dalai Lama to the left, and, in the middle, Pope John Paul II. The World Day of Prayer for Peace was John Paul's idea, and while it had been choreographed, in accordance with Catholic doctrine, to set him off distinctly from the others, the photographs in the next day's papers showed him standing in the group as one religious leader among many. It was a sight without precedent in the long history of the papacy, and it led some traditionalist Catholics to denounce John Paul as a pope flirting with heresy. But it opened a door; and with the door open, the pope stepped aside to let Sant'Egidio carry the event forward, making the Community an advance guard for peacemaking and interreligious dialogue.

The Community was itself diverse in its makeup and interreligious in program, and this came to be reflected vividly in the annual Prayer for Peace, held each year in a different city: Warsaw, Brussels, Milan, Jerusalem.

Its projects across Rome were well established: welcome centers for immigrants, and the elderly, and "schools of peace" in poor neighborhoods. As the movement spread across Italy and beyond, so did its sense of the *periferia*, which was deepened by Riccardi's sense of history and other members' growing experience in government and politics. For them, diplomacy came naturally as a tool to reduce poverty (since "war is the mother of all poverties"), and in time their gifts were put to the test. At the invitation of some Mozambicans who came to Rome, Riccardi and others went to Maputo, that country's capital, bringing food and aid packages, because the combined effect of the country's long civil war and a famine was destroying the country. In Maputo it was apparent that, without peace, no amount of aid would be enough. So Sant'Egidio invited Mozambican government officials and leaders of the opposition guerrilla movement to come to Rome for peace talks—and they came, surprising everybody. When, after twenty-six months of intermittent talks, they emerged from the old convent in October 1992 with a peace accord, *Le Monde* on its front page announced a

"Pax Romana;" soon the Italian press dubbed Sant'Egidio "the United Nations of Trastevere."

What made this peace possible? Riccardi, and Mario with him, speak of "weak strength," which they say is inspired by group's original idea about the gospel and friendship—the impulse "to start from what unites and not from what divides people," as "good Pope John" XXIII used to say. It may sound vague, but it works: it invites people who are nominally adversaries to come together through friends in common. This requires a spirit of friendship, yes—but also cultural awareness, flexibility, a willingness to set aside vested interests, an eye for opportunities within seeming obstacles, attention to the human factor, and lots of hard work.

Likewise the community's method of organization. There is an elected president and an executive board, but few other members claim formal titles. They take different roles as needed. Andrea Riccardi—now a professor of church history—has served (post-Berlusconi) as the Italians government's minister for human rights, paying special attention to the rights of the tens of thousands of *migranti* coming to Italy by ramshackle boats from North Africa. Daniela Pompei is renowned as an advocate for immigrants and their rights. Claudio Betti, a teacher fluent in English, is a presence for Sant'Egidio in North America; so are the husband-and-wife team of Andrea Bartoli and Paola Piscitelli, he as dean of the foreign service school at Seton Hall University in New Jersey, and she as the organizer of a nascent Sant'Egidio community house on Stuyvesant Square in Manhattan and a Christmas meal for the poor akin to the one in Trastevere.

The friends who founded Sant'Egidio are European eminences now. They receive honorary degrees and prizes from UNESCO and other groups; they are invited to speak worldwide; they write opinion columns for *La Vanguardia* and the *Corriere della Sera*. The Christmas dinner is now offered in sixty countries to some 150,000 guests. The annual Prayer for Peace—held in recent years in Krakow, Munich, Sarajevo, and Antwerp—draws several thousand participants from the full spread of religious traditions. The lighting of the Colosseum when a country rejects the death penalty is covered by the press in Italian, Spanish, French, Portuguese, and English, and in five languages on the movement's website, www.santegidio.org. Georgetown University was the first North American host of the Prayer for Peace, in Washington, DC, and the university's president, John J. DeGioia, takes part in the annual event wherever it is held. Princeton University has students learn about the movement during a summer course in Rome. When the US Secretary of State travels to Rome, a meeting with Sant'Egidio often takes place.

Some months after his election, Pope Francis came over from the Vatican and spent two hours at Santa Maria in Trastevere with the Community and the poor. The streets of the neighborhood, always crowded, were absolutely jammed. The occasion was not Mass, but unique "communion event," in which Francis's teachings on the role of mercy and the value of friendship with the poor and seemed naturally akin to the Community's own efforts and outlook.

In 2014 Francis followed John Paul II and Benedict XVI in denouncing the death penalty as a violation of civilized norms and our common humanity. It was the strongest statement against the death penalty the church has ever made.

Mario Marazziti turned sixty not long ago. His business cards identify him as a Deputato in the Camera dei Deputati. He remains a genius of friendship and an enthusiast for whatever it is the Community is doing to make the world a more humane and livable place. He'll mention a plan to bring Wine for Life to the United States in the form of a tie-in with Newman's Own salad dressing. Or he'll hint at Sant'Egidio's back-channel role in creating a "bridge" to end the violence in Syria and make a political solution possible. As we step out into the Roman night, the flats dark above the thronged *trattorie*, he'll talk about a plan for Sant'Egidio's members in Rome to reach out the city's elderly in the summertime, visiting them and performing simple tasks so as to keep shut-ins from dying in a heat wave as Europe feels the effects of climate change. "One of our people goes to the top of the stairs with a bag of groceries or gives the doorman a few euros to do it," he explains. The effort to form networks of neighbors has become a "pilot program" funded by the

Italian government, with an eye to spreading it throughout the European Union as an antidote to the loneliness of many elderly people and an alternative to the costly impersonal approach of most social programs. Compared with lighting up the Colosseum or fighting AIDS—or bringing the death penalty to an end worldwide—it's no big deal. But as he describes it, it seems not only simple but natural and necessary, one more way for people to be friends to one another.

Notes

1. David Edwards, "New Evidence Could Clear 14-Year-Old Executed by South Carolina," *Raw Story*, October 3, 2011, http://www.rawstory.com/rs/2011/10/new-evidence-could-clear-14-year-old-executed-by-south-carolina/.
2. Ibid.
3. US Department of Justice, Office of Justice Programs, *Capital Punishment, 2012—Statistics Tables*, 2012, http://www.deathpenaltyinfo.org/documents/cp12st.pdf.
4. Bill Mears, "High Court: Juvenile Death Penalty Unconstitutional," *CNN.com*, March 1, 2005, http://www.cnn.com/2005/LAW/03/01/scotus.death.penalty/index.html?iref=mpstoryview.
5. "The Death Penalty for Juveniles," *Capital Punishment in Context*, http://www.capitalpunishmentincontext.org/issues/juveniles.
6. Phyllis L. Crocker, "Childhood Abuse and Adult Murder: Implications for the Death Penalty," *North Carolina Law Review* 77:1143 (1999), http://engagedscholarship.csuohio.edu/cgi/viewcontent.cgi?article=1278&context=fac_articles.
7. "US Executions from 1608–2002," ProCon.org, January 7, 2011, http://deathpenalty.procon.org/view.resource.php?resourceID=004087.
8. Ibid.
9. Ibid.
10. Ibid.
11. Ibid.
12. "Shrinking Majority of Americans Support Death Penalty," Pew Research, March 28, 2014, http://www.pewforum.org/2014/03/28/shrinking-majority-of-americans-support-death-penalty/.

13. Ibid.
14. "Facts About the Death Penalty," Death Penalty Information Center, January 22, 2015, http://www.deathpenaltyinfo.org/documents/FactSheet.pdf.
15. "The Death Penalty in 2013: Year End Report," Death Penalty Information Center, http://deathpenaltyinfo.org/documents/YearEnd2013.pdf.
16. "Death Penalty 101," American Civil Liberties Union, October 3, 2011, https://www.aclu.org/capital-punishment/death-penalty-101.
17. Ibid.
18. "Death Penalty and Mental Illness," Amnesty International, http://www.amnestyusa.org/our-work/issues/death-penalty/us-death-penalty-facts/death-penalty-and-mental-illness.
19. "States without the Death Penalty," Death Penalty Information Center, http://www.deathpenaltyinfo.org/states-and-without-death-penalty.
20. Sandra Babcock, "Death Row Conditions," Death Penalty Information Center, last updated June 2008; state by state comparison of conditions.
21. Ibid.
22. "The Death Penalty in 2013: Year End Report," Death Penalty Information Center.
23. Ibid.
24. Office of Performance Evaluations Idaho Legislature, *Financial Costs of the Death Penalty*, March 2014, http://www.legislature.idaho.gov/ope/publications/reports/r1402.pdf.
25. Ibid.
26. Andrew Knittle, "Oklahoma to Continue Last Meal Tradition for Condemned Inmates," *News OK*, September 27, 2011, http://newsok.com/oklahoma-to-continue-last-meal-tradition-for-condemned-inmates/article/3607859.
27. Molly Hennessy-Fisk, "Texas Ends 'Last Meals' for Death Row Inmates" *Los Angeles Times*, September 23, 2011, http://latimesblogs.latimes.com/nationnow/2011/09/texas-ends-death-row-inmates-final-meals.html.

28. Michael L. Radelet, "Examples of Post-*Furman* Botched Executions," Death Penalty Information Center, last addition July 24, 2014, http://www.deathpenaltyinfo.org/some-examples-post-furman-botched-executions?scid=8&did=478#_edn3.

29. "Part I: History of the Death Penalty," Death Penalty Information Center, http://www.deathpenaltyinfo.org/part-i-history-death-penalty.

30. *Wilkerson v. Utah*, 99 US 130 (1878), http://caselaw.lp.findlaw.com/scripts/getcase.pl?court=us&vol=99&invol=130.

31. "Death Sentences and Executions 2013 Report," Amnesty International, March 26, 2014, http://www.amnestyusa.org/research/reports/death-sentences-and-executions-2013, Saudi Arabia.

32. Ibid., United States.

33. Ibid., Iran, Kuwait, Somalia, United Arab Emirates.

34. Ibid.

35. "Death Penalty for Offenses other than Murder," Death Penalty Information Center, http://www.deathpenaltyinfo.org/death-penalty-offenses-other-murder.

36. "The Last Public Execution in America," *National Public Radio Morning Edition*, May 1, 2001, http://www.npr.org/programs/morning/features/2001/apr/010430.execution.html.

37. "Timeline of Capital Punishment in Britain," Capital Punishment UK, http://www.capitalpunishmentuk.org/timeline.html.

38. Ibid.

39. "Death Sentences and Executions Report," Amnesty International, March 26, 2014, Iran, North Korea, Saudi Arabia, Somalia.

40. Greg Bluestein, "Georgia's Videotaped Execution Sets New Precedent," Associated Press, July 22, 2011, http://law.fordham.edu/faculty/23070.htm.

41. Mark D. Cunningham, PhD and Mark P. Vigen, PhD, "Death Row Inmate Characteristics, Adjustment, and Confinement: A Critical Review of the Literature," *Behavioral Sciences and*

the Law 20 (2002): 191–210, http://www.deathpenaltyinfo. org/documents/CunninghamDeathRowReview.pdf.

42. US Department of Justice, Office of Justice Programs, *Capital Punishment, 2009—Statistical Tables*, 2009, http://www. bjs.gov/content/pub/pdf/cp09st.pdf.

43. "US Executions from 1608–2002," ProCon.org.

44. Ibid.

45. Jocelyn M. Pollock *Women's Crimes, Criminology, and Corrections* (Long Grove, IL: Waveland Press, 2014).

46. Catherine Fisher Collins, *The Imprisonment of African American Women: Causes, Experiences, and Effects* (Jefferson, NC: McFarland, 2010).

47. Belarus, Guatemala, Mongolia, Russia, and Tajikistan, see "Death Penalty Worldwide," Cornell University Law School, updated January 25, 2012, http://www.deathpenaltyworldwide.org/women.cfm.

48. Ibid.

49. St. Kitts and Nevis, see "Death Penalty Worldwide," Cornell University Law School.

50. "Member States of the United Nations," United Nations, http://www.un.org/en/members/.

51. Ibid.

52. "Death Row Inmates, 1953–2009," ProCon.org, updated September 26, 2011, http://deathpenalty.procon.org/view. resource.php?resourceID=004433.

53. Ibid.

54. David Lester PhD and Christine Tartaro PhD, "Suicide on Death Row," *Journal of Forensic Sciences* 47, no. 5 (2002), http://www.hawaii.edu/hivandaids/Suicide_on_Death_Row. pdf#.

55. "Innocence: List of Those Freed From Death Row," Death Penalty Information Center, updated December 9, 2014, http://www.deathpenaltyinfo.org/innocence-list-those-freed-death-row?scid=6&did=110.

56. John H. Blume, "Killing the Willing: 'Volunteers,' Suicide and Competency," 103 *Michigan Law Review* 939 (2005)

http://www.deathpenaltyinfo.org/documents/BlumeVolunteerArticle.pdf.

57. Ibid.

58. Richard C. Dieter, Esq., "With Justice for Few: The Growing Crisis in Death Penalty Representation," Death Penalty Information Center, October 1995, http://www.deathpenaltyinfo.org/node/742.

59. Ibid.

60. Sanford, Florida resident Zimmerman was acquitted of second-degree murder charges in July 2013, as a jury concluded that Zimmerman's infamous fatal shooting of teenager Trayvon Martin was done in self-defense. See Rene Stutzman and Jeff Weiner, "Zimmerman's Not-Guilty Verdict Comes with 'Mind-numbing' $2.5M Bill," *Orlando Sentinel*, November 29, 2013, http://www.orlandosentinel.com/news/trayvon-martin-george-zimmerman/os-george-zimmerman-legal-bills-20131129-story.html.

61. Ibid.

62. "US Man Freed by DNA Evidence After 35 Years in Prison," *BBC News*, December 18, 2009, http://news.bbc.co.uk/2/hi/americas/8419854.stm; David Reutter, "Florida Prisoner Exonerated by DNA After Serving 35 Years," *Prison Legal News*, June 2010, https://www.prisonlegalnews.org/news/2010/jun/15/florida-prisoner-exonerated-by-dna-after-serving-35-years/.

63. Ibid.

64. "Eyewitness Misidentification," *Innocence Project*, http://www.innocenceproject.org/understand/Eyewitness-Misidentification.php.

65. Brandon L. Garrett, *Convicting the Innocent* (Cambridge, MA: Harvard University Press, 2011), 281; see also "Eyewitness Misidentifications," University of Virginia School of Law, http://www.law.virginia.edu/html/librarysite/garrett_eyewitness.htm.

66. Following 11 years in TDCJ overseeing the information center and media relations, Michelle Lyons was demoted from direc-

tor of public information to public information officer, after TDCJ wrongly accused her of "keeping inaccurate time." She sued the administration that had cut her salary and suspended her for five days and put her on probation for nine months. She accused her bosses of retaliating against her for having answered a media inquiry from a blogger about the strict control the administration exerts over employees. A brutal epilogue for a woman that has served the administration defending the system "no matter what," and a dark light on the tensions inside the Texas Department of Criminal Justice.

67. Ruth Massingill, Ardyth Broadrick Sohn, *Prison City* (New York: Peter Lang Publishing, 2007), 127. An account is given of the last three days of a convict's life, taken from the media kit prepared for the press.

April 18, 2005

12:44 a.m.	Inmate sleeping
6:02 a.m.	Inmate standing at cell door
8:22 a.m.	Inmate arrived at visitation
11:37 a.m.	Inmate visiting and eating
5:06 p.m.	Inmate escorted back to the cell from visitation
8:31 p.m.	Inmate showering
10:57 p.m.	Inmate sleeping

April 19, 2005

12:04 a.m.	Inmate sleeping
3:29 a.m.	Inmate eating breakfast
7:26 a.m.	Inmate standing at cell door talking
8:05 a.m.	Inmate escorted to visitation
12:38 p.m.	Inmate visiting
4:40 p.m.	Inmate visiting
6:46 p.m.	Inmate standing at cell door
8:30 p.m.	Inmate reading and opening small mail
11:30 p.m.	Inmate sleeping

April 20, 2005

12:02 a.m.	Inmate sleeping
2:44 a.m.	Inmate sorting mail

4:30 a.m.	Inmate reading mail
8:01 a.m.	Inmate is packing property
8:25 a.m.	Inmate escorted to visitation
9:06 a.m.	Inmate eating and visiting
12:00 p.m.	Inmate visitation terminated

68. Other groups included Murder Victims' Families for Human Rights; the US National Coalition; Death Penalty Focus, the organization in California coordinated at the time by Lance Lindsay and Mike Farrell; and the National Association of Criminal Defense Lawyers (NACDL), engaged through the good offices of human rights activist and legal scholar Speedy Rice.

69. On September 22, 2006, Fabianus Tibo, Dominggus da Silva and Marinus Riwu, three Indonesian Catholics, were put to death in Palu, Indonesia. Former Indonesian president Abdurrahman Wahid had just a few days earlier renewed his plea to suspend the execution and reopen the trial, which had been decided without the testimony of many defense witnesses being heard. He joined the voices of other Muslim representatives who, during the International Peace Conference in Assisi organized by the Community of Sant'Egidio, had asked Indonesian Head of State Susilo Bambang Yudhoyono to intervene on the prisoners' behalf. In the months preceding the execution of the three men, the Community of Sant'Egidio worked closely with the movement to save their lives, including their legal defense team, their prison chaplain Monsignor Joseph Suwatan, and the Indonesian Episcopal Conference. A widespread movement sprang up in support of them. The European Union, the Italian government, and prominent state figures from Germany and Spain became involved. In addition, Pope Benedict XVI, who had often spoken about the case, made a personal appeal for a pardon to the Indonesian president on August 11, 2006.

70. The Justice Ministers of the following countries took part in the talks sponsored by the Community of Sant'Egidio, starting from the first round on November 28, 2005: Togo, Burkina Faso, Benin, Cameroon, Democratic Republic of

the Congo, Congo Brazzaville, Madagascar, Kenya, Malawi, South Africa, Ghana, Tanzania, Burundi, Morocco, Senegal, Ivory Coast, Mozambique, Liberia, Lesotho, Rwanda, Central African Republic, Gabon, Gambia, Niger, and Ethiopia.

About the Author

MARIO MARAZZITI co-founded the World Coalition Against the Death Penalty in 2002. He is known internationally as the spokesperson for the Community of Sant'Egidio, a progressive Catholic movement devoted to peacemaking and human rights, based in Rome and present in seventy countries. He is also a longtime a contributing writer to *Corriere della Sera*. In 2012 he was elected to the lower House of Parliament in Italy, where he pursues a broad human-rights portfolio. He lives in Rome.

Georgetown University's Berkley Center for Religion, Peace, and World Affairs senior fellow Paul Elie is the author of *The Life You Save May Be Your Own* (2003) and *Reinventing Bach* (2012), both National Book Critics Circle Award finalists, and a contributor to *The Atlantic*, *Vanity Fair*, and *The New York Times Book Review*. He posts pieces daily to everythingthatrises.com.